Managing Mindfully

BOOK ONE : A MINDFUL APPROACH TO TIME MANAGEMENT

Tom Evans

Tmesis Ltd

Surrey UK

Managing Time Mindfully

A Mindful Approach to Time Management

Practical Mindfulness Book One

ISBN : 978-1-849148603

Copyright © 2015 Tom Evans and Tmesis Ltd

First Edition 2015

Contents

to Louise for all of the time you shared with me

0 : About Time

THIS IS A BOOK ABOUT TIME. MORE SPECIFICALLY, IT'S A BOOK ABOUT OUR RELATIONSHIP TO IT.

So many people claim to be time poor these days, asking for an extra hour a day or another day a week. I suspect some people use the lack of time for not-getting-things-done. Yet, as you will see, this enslavement from time is one of our own making.

This is rather good news as, if we have created something, we can deconstruct it and build it up again to better serve us.

I should say from the outset that this book does not advocate that we get rid of time. Our modern society needs us to 'keep' time so we can ensure we get to places 'on time' and 'in time'. We want our aeroplanes, trains, ships, and buses to run on time and not to 'arrive' at destinations at exactly the same time. We also want to be to able measure time exactly so that we can find out who is the fastest over 100 metres.

This is a different book than the one I planned originally. Just as I was about to start writing it in earnest, an unexpected encounter with a black labrador called Henry and my knee resulted in a leg break. A 'break' of a different kind ensued as I ended up with more time on my hands than expected or intended. This made me 'think' deeply about the nature of time. Again, more specifically, it lead to me 'not-thinking' about it and meditating upon what time really was and where it came from. As a result, elements from the first quarter of this book, and all of the last quarter, although not in my original plan, have snuck into the book.

From as long as I can remember, I noticed that different people seem to think and react to the world at different speeds. I wondered if we might all experience the world at 'pass by' faster or slower than each other. A fly, for example, avoids being swatted because the signals from its neurons don't take long to get to its brain. It can 'see' us coming. By the way, I gave up swatting flies long ago and now just encourage them to fly out of a window.

Two people waiting for an appointment in a doctor's surgery might see the delay differently. One might be absorbed with looking at their emails on their smartphone. The other might be engaged in 'self-talk'; worried about their affliction and the doctor's impending prognosis.

Time, as you will see and probably know already, is subjective. Time also needs an observer, as Einstein observed, and is relative to that observer.

My fascination with time began in my mid-forties, on and around the time I began to meditate. Before I learned how to make my mind go quiet, I laboured under the opinion that meditation was one big waste of time. I was a busy guy with things to do and places to go. I had been given a sales target although I hadn't taken this particular job on in a sales role. They found I was good at it—probably because I took the time to understand what the customer wanted.

The job stressed me out, though, and I began to take 10 — 20 minutes out most mornings before setting off to work. Quickly, I discovered that days went more smoothly on the days I meditated, and had more tendency to go awry when I didn't. I went for walks at lunchtime on days I couldn't meditate first thing.

As a result of this practice, I ended up leaving that job and, after a few false starts with other enterprises, fell into a new career as an author and author's mentor. At this point, my relationship with time altered significantly. By the way, I am sharing this here as I feel I should emphasise that my experience with time is empirical and not theoretical.

I went on a few self-development courses, mainly so I could better help writers get through creative blocks. I learned how to get into a 'no time' space where time seemed to elongate to fit the task at hand. I experienced 'future memories' and learned how to tap into them. I found that I could 'see' through time and use this 'different-ability' to heal 'dis-eases' of both the mind and body. I also discovered that everybody 'so minded' can do this too.

I also experienced that when time 'stops', our relationship with gravity alters such that we are able to levitate. I even interviewed someone on my podcast who had experienced this happening.

If it sounds at this point that I have gone off the rails, and you've picked up a book written by a madman, please bear with me and the book. The fundamental aim of the book is to help you get more done with less time. You will also learn how to allow events to unfold at just the perfect time with less stress and effort.

My unexpected leg break, a week before going on what was to be a walking holiday, is a good example of this. I had planned to write a book that just explained how to use mindfulness meditation techniques to get more done in less time. On reflection, it dawned upon me that it was 'high time' that I wrote a more comprehensive exploration of our relationship with time.

In meditation, an alternative structure for the book came to me than the one I had previously mapped out pre-leg-break. Our hours are split into quarters and our years into seasons. We have 12 months in each year and use a 12-hour clock. Accordingly, this book is comprised of four quarters, each containing three chapters.

First Quarter : First Tickings

Chapter 1 : Where Does the Time Go?
I start the book exploring why we are so time poor these days.

Chapter 2 : When Time Began
To really understand time, we have to go right back to what we know about when it first started.

Chapter 3 : The Hands of Time
I then explain how time, as modern-day humans know it and count it, came about.

Second Quarter : Perceptions of Time

Chapter 4 : Two Minds of Time
Bizarrely, it transpires that parts of our brain experience the passage of time differently.

Chapter 5 : Whole Mind Time
Furthermore, different parts of our neurology also have a different relationship with time.

Chapter 6 : Stretching Time
We can use this knowledge and engage in mindfulness techniques that expand time.

Third Quarter : Managing Time

Chapter 7 : Me Time
Fundamental to managing time mindfully is a change in our personal relationship with it.

Chapter 8 : Natural Time
Our man-made calendars cause us to lose sync with time. This chapter explains how to go with the temporal flow.

Chapter 9 : Just in Time
When we regain control of time, something magical happens. External events start to occur at just the perfect time.

Fourth Quarter : Temporal Alchemy

Chapter 10 : Passed Lives
The past makes us who we are today and forms who we will be tomorrow. It can also hold us back and prevent us from shining our true light.

Chapter 11 : Future Entanglement
Time's forward arrow is an illusion. We can tap into the future to help us in our creative and business endeavours.

Chapter 12 : Down the Rabbit Hole
This last chapter explores some of the more bizarre temporal happenings that I have come across. All of them are true, virtually none of them are provable, but I share them and invite you to get in touch if any of them has happened to you.

Timeful Tasks

At the end of each quarter, you will find a simple timeful task. These are natural pauses to encourage you to think about your relationship with time. They are small encouragements to consider time as a resource that is to be invested and spent, rather than something that passes us by inexorably.

Temporally Yours,

Tom Evans, The Surrey Hills, UK—Autumn, 2015

Tom Evans

quarter 1

first
tickings

I : Where Does the Time Go?

EVERYTHING IS IN CONSTANT MOTION.

Unless you are on the International Space Station, or at one of the poles, the ground under your feet is moving at over 1000 miles an hour. For every hour that passes, the Earth moves over 67,000 miles through space. Each and every year, we all travel over half a billion miles around the Sun together.

The Sun itself is moving at 450,000 miles an hour around the centre of our galaxy and, along with our home planet, so are we.

It is perhaps no wonder that we feel a little rushed some days.

Now, it might be somewhat ironic, but we spend little time thinking about time and how we use it. The world has gone 24x7, yet we don't give a second thought as to even why there are only 24 hours in each day.

These days, so many people seem to be afflicted by a kind of temporal malaise, where they constantly complain that there is not enough time and that there are just not enough hours in the day.

We are indoctrinated with the notion of time from birth. Babies have times for feeding, changing, and bathing. Timetables regulate our school lessons. School-time all too quickly morphs into the nine to five of work-time. We intersperse our days with breakfast times, break times, lunch times, tea times, and supper times. Commuters just have to catch that train, right on time.

We have a bedtime and, before we know it, it's time to get up again. Note that between these two times, when we are sleeping and dreaming, time takes on a different and ethereal quality. If you ever end up awake in the small hours, however, time can seem to stretch to eternity.

Our language, too, is littered with temporal references:

'Just a minute.'
'Give me a second.'
'Cometh the hour, cometh the man.'
'Clocking in late; clocking off early.'
'That is so last season.'
'Holding back the years.'

Time is imposed upon us from birth right through to death, and we cannot escape either its forward arrow or its grip.

Stop the World, I Want to Get Off

In our so-called modern society, what is making this somewhat worse is that the world is permanently 'switched on'. Before we had electric light, people snuffed out candles and went to sleep when it got dark.

When I was born, in the late 1950s, the UK had only two TV channels. Neither transmitted programmes after midnight, and they started up only when people came home from work. By the time I graduated from university and got my dream job as an engineer at the BBC at the end of the 70s, TV broadcast in glorious Technicolor, and satellite TV had literally taken off.

Wind the clock on by just a few decades to today and we are now overloaded with information. In the UK alone, our four terrestrial TV channels have morphed into hundreds of digital channels. Some of them repeat themselves an hour later. Many of them can be tapped into 'on demand'.

Unless you are at the bottom of a gold mine, every minute of every day, their electromagnetic signals pass through your body unnoticed, along with thousands of radio channels, mobile phone calls, and text messages. It's lucky we are not tuned in to them.

What's more, we have all become broadcasters, or narrowcasters at least, over the Internet. If you have a smartphone or tablet, you can generate news as it happens, do a funny dance that goes viral, or post a message online to change hearts and minds.

Every month a new service seems to launch to allow us to share content with others. YouTube is now one of the most watched 'TV channels' on the planet, and we all generate, curate, and share its content.

Our 'smart devices' are our windows into this virtual world. The ubiquitous availability of high-speed broadband and mobile data networks means that we are always connected. Each year, more and more of us generate and consume more and more data. It's estimated that over two billion people own a mobile device.

People even take their phones and that different type of tablet to bed these days. Many check their email, Facebook page, and Twitter feed before retiring and upon waking. Some enterprising therapists now make a living by treating people so afflicted with email, computer games, and social media addictions. An unwanted side effect of social media is that it can somewhat ironically cause us to be antisocial.

To get an idea of the scale of information overload, this is how our data generation per capita per year has grown in less than thirty years. In 1986, the data we generated and that was stored about us could fit on a single CD-ROM.

These days, on average, we are each filling up the equivalent of a 256GB data card each year with photos, videos, email, and podcasts. Fortunately, while the data we all generate has increased exponentially, thankfully the physical size of storage has decreased in inverse proportion.

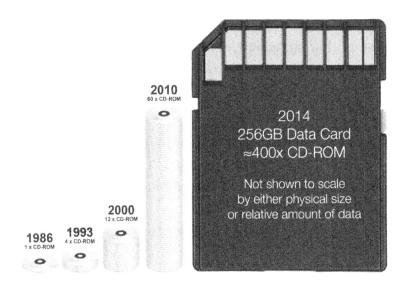

So, nowadays, two billion connected people generate two zettabytes of information per year. That's 2,000,000,000,000,000,000,000 bytes, which is much more than we could ever hope to chew!

To understand how much we all form part of this collective problem, it is worth thinking about our contribution to this media mountain. Our daily output of emails not only takes us time to generate but consumes time for others who read and respond to them. Consider this:

• Roughly how many emails do you send a day?
• If you are on social media, how many posts do you do?
• On your camera or smartphone, how many pictures do you take and share?
• Do you produce audio podcasts or Youtube videos?

Living Timefully

Like all human advancements, there are good and not so good ramifications to this vast media mountain. My personal view is that the benefits outweigh any negatives. For example, I was able to research some of the data for this book from the comfort of my sofa, with my trusty iPad. The manuscript ebbed and flowed to and from my editor via email. The print and ebook files found their way to online book repositories over the Internet.

Many readers of the print version of the book may have sampled it and purchased it without taking time out to go to a book shop. Increasingly more people just download books onto e-readers, smartphones, and tablets. From the reduced consumption of fossil fuels alone, this is a good thing. Most importantly, of course, it saved me loads of time and allowed the book to come out in not much time at all when compared to publishing methods of only half a century ago.

Like all tools, the Internet can be used to save time or waste time. Some people, though, choose to spend their days looking down and out of what we call reality into a virtual world. This man-made netherworld is full of angry birds, trolls, spammers, 'bots, and even some nasty viruses. The Internet should be our slave, and we can choose not to be enslaved by it. Likewise, we can turn the TV off at any time, use it to turn our minds off, or use it for education or entertainment.

The choices are ours.

When we are mindful about how we utilise our time, we can find that there are actually enough hours in the day. We discover, too, an easier and smarter way to go about our days where external events seem to happen in just the right time. The secret to living such a charmed existence lies in taking control of your Personal Time Machine—your mind—or, as you will see, more specifically your minds.

People who live a time-full existence are super-productive, super-creative, and also super-lucky. They always land on their feet. For them, the glass isn't so much half full but positively overflowing. As a result, they not only seem to have time to get done all they want done but seem to have an amazing capacity to help others.

While being 'time-full' is an initiative we undertake from an individual and personal perspective, it is also scalable and has commercial applications.

When whole businesses work time-fully, they get more done than their competitors, in less time. They take action more quickly and are always quicker out of the block and more reactive to market conditions and opportunities. They spend less time in meetings and more time making things happen and in front of customers. Their employees are happier, too, and are less prone to take days off with illness or to change jobs.

So what are the keys to living such a life?

It lies in understanding how the perception of the passage time is created by where and how we direct our attention. If we lose focus from the task in hand, then our efficiency drops.

By using simple mindfulness techniques, our minds can become immune from the distractions and bandits of time that are sent to plague us. When we live a timeful existence, we are able to jump outside linear time, and tasks seem to get done within the time we have allocated to them.

This has some amazing spin-offs as it reduces stress and improves health and vitality. In turn, taking less time off work increases overall productivity and leads to higher creative output.

By taking a fundamentally different and innovative approach to time management, we can change our minds and the nature of our thoughts so that we get more done in less time.

On the surface, this feat might seem as if it's magic, but there are no arcane secrets here, and no sleight-of-mind. In any event, any magic trick ceases to be magic once we know how it's done. We can create more time just using simple and practical techniques that can be learned by everyone, with ease.

Give It to a Busy Person

Maybe you've seen and admired those people who seem to get so much done and wondered how they pack it into their days. Perhaps they are insomniacs and never sleep. Maybe they have a 25th hour secreted away somewhere in each of their days.

This book will lift the lid on how such seemingly busy people get in and stay in their creative and productive zones.

Quite rightly, most conventional time management systems focus on goal setting, intelligent prioritisation, and improved interruption management. When we see time as being linear and a finite resource, with a forward arrow, this is a good strategy.

There are some good books and fabulous resources out there. I am not advocating that we replace conventional time management techniques, so there is no need to throw away your best practices and learn a new system. Everything you find here merely augments existing practices.

Although time, with its forward arrow, does tick relentlessly forwards, remarkably it is both malleable and stretchable. We have all experienced this phenomenon.

If you have a busy day at the office, the hours can fly by and, before you know it, you ask where the time went. If you are waiting for the phone to ring, perhaps when a customer promised to call with a sales order, minutes can stretch into hours. The perceived passage of time is subjective. The reason for this seeming paradox is that the nature and content of our thoughts, and the state of our consciousness, have an effect on how we experience time.

To many people, though, the thought of having unlimited time might cause a problem. The lack of time is the perfect excuse for not getting things done. Some people might even fear that their positions would be under threat. Others may be concerned that there would be nothing left to strive for if their dreams were fulfilled.

So, if we had a magical way of generating more time, there would be no let off and no way out. Our 'To Do' lists would have to get done!

The key to taking time back under our control lies in gaining an understanding of where time came from in the first place.

II : When Time Began

TO BECOME TRULY MINDFUL ABOUT HOW WE SPEND AND INVEST OUR TIME, IT HELPS IF WE GET AN UNDERSTANDING ABOUT WHAT TIME IS AND WHERE IT CAME FROM.

This might sound like scaling a mountain rather than tackling a molehill, but it is a fundamental undertaking if we truly desire to change our relationship with time.

This chapter might, at first, sound overly scientific in scope, so I have done my best to keep it simple and descriptive.

Our astronomers and cosmologists have done the most fabulous detective work. Over the last few hundred years, they have identified our place in the Universe, in both space and time. As light takes time to traverse the Universe, we can look 'back in time' and still 'see' elements of the early Universe and work out what it was made from. The 'smoking gun' of what is thought to be the beginning of space and time, the Big Bang, has even been detected.

The reason this is possible is thought to be that the Universe is expanding, and the speed of light is relatively fixed. So, for example, when we see the Sun, which is 93 million miles away, we see it just over 8 minutes 'late'. The light from the nearest stars gets to us just over four years after it left. Given a sensitive enough telescope, looking at the right part of the spectrum, we can now see back over 13 billion years ago in time.

This is an amazing achievement for science. What is also significant, as you will discover in the 4th quarter of this book, is that 'all time' exists at the same time. As our minds are part of the Universe too, we just have to tune them in to 'when' we want.

Cosmic Yardsticks

Apparently, we live on a small rock that we call the Earth, which spins on its axis once a day. Our Spaceship Earth revolves around a medium-sized star once in what we call a year. This star is either a third or fourth generation star. This means two or three sets of stars before it have exploded in cataclysmic supernovae. The remnants of these star deaths have re-coalesced to make our Sun, its planets, and Us. Yes, we are literally star dust.

Our star sits on the spiral arm of a galaxy at about 27,000 light-years from its centre. Our galaxy is what we call the Milky Way. It is around 100,000 light years across and contains around 400 billion other stars. Our galaxy is one of billions of other galaxies—the nearest being Andromeda, which is around 2.5 million light years away. The Universe is massive!

It is 'guestimated' that the whole visible Universe we see today came from 'no-thing' in a Big Bang about 13 —14 billion years ago. That was one hell of a bang which, incidentally, made no sound at all and had nobody around to hear it.

What's interesting about this model is that we use a local and variable yardstick to measure and help us get our head around it all. We use the notion of a year. For starters, our Earth years have varied over time as the Earth's orbit has altered. Secondly, go to another planet, like Mars, and years are around double of ours. Lastly, Earth years did not even exist at all for the majority of the life of the Universe.

This is a bit like measuring the height of a tree using a whole load of paperclips, of varying sizes. Apart from it being a little impractical, you would only be measuring half of the tree anyway by ignoring its root system.

In passing, I should mention that the light-year, the distance that light travels in a year, is also a little arbitrary in its use as a cosmic yardstick. The speed of light changes under gravity and has changed over time as the Universe has become less dense.

Referencing the whole of creation using a local time constant, (which is not that constant) though, does allow us at least to get our heads around the enormity of the Universe we live in.

First Light

Before the first stars formed, 'time-as-we-know-it' did not exist. Only when nuclear processes really fired up did the components of the Universe 'have' any sense of one event leading to another event. For a time after the Big Bang, the Universe remained totally dark and had no light at all.

Cosmologists postulate that First Light, as they call it, came 380,000 years after the Big Bang. As there was no Earth with no years with which to measure it, putting any length of time on that period is somewhat nonsensical and meaningless. A better way entirely to describe this period is that everything from the Big Bang to First Light happened at the same time.

During this 'time', elementary particles were 'working out' how to form the matter that we are all made from. When enough of this new matter coalesced, it expanded greatly and exploded in a burst of light. At around this 'time', the three dimensions of space and one dimension of time were created. Before then, there was really no 'up', 'down', or 'sideways', and not much of a 'when' either. As the matter and light streamed out, they formed the cosmos we see today and what is called the backdrop of the 'space-time' continuum over which we experience our lives.

The first generation of stars emerged relatively quickly from this First Light and shone brightly. They formed primarily from hydrogen and helium and only lived for a few million years. They contain none of the heavy elements that we are made from.

Although, measuring their life in years is a little academic, as there were no planets around and 'time-as-we-know-it' today still did not exist for such a star. While the dimension of time existed, with no observer or yardsticks, the notion of any passage time was somewhat academic.

When these stars exploded and made second generation stars, some of these stars captured gaseous 'nearly stars' that then rotated around them. If you were around then on one of these stars, only then may you have been able to count 'days' and 'years' as the planets rotated on their axis and around their 'foster parent' of a star.

Only when this second generation of stars exploded, did heavier elements form—such as atoms like silicon, and metals that rocky planets like the Earth are made from. The fourth most abundant element of the Universe was also made at this time, which is the carbon that life on Earth is based upon. Incidentally, the third most abundant element in the Universe is oxygen.

These heavier elements formed into accretion discs around the next generation of stars that look like a giant pair of fried eggs sandwiched together. The heavier elements in these discs subsequently coalesced into rocky planets like the Earth. Gases formed planets like Jupiter and Saturn. If you were to look down from above at one of these rotating discs, you would have seen what looked like a large spinning clock face. The rotating planets had started to mark out time.

First Time

It took around 10 billion Earth years after the Big Bang before solar systems, like ours, with heavy rocky planets formed.

Let's just imagine for a moment that out of all the planets around all the stars in all the galaxies, life-as-we-know-it took hold on just one planet. Of course, this does sound ridiculous if you think about it.

Anyhow, on good old planet Earth, a billion years or so after it formed, around 3 billion of our years ago, something rather magical happened. Around some super-hot volcanic vents deep at the bottom of the ocean, some molecules got 'clever' and learned to replicate themselves. The successful molecules got their timing right too. They 'knew' when to replicate and when to die. Those that chose the most optimum timing thrived, and the ones that were 'out of time' faded away.

The most successful of the conglomerations of molecules then learned when to evolve to more complex life forms. As sunlight may not have penetrated to these depths of the ocean, they would have been working to few external temporal references.

I should stress that this part of the model of how life gained a foothold, as well as the cosmology above, is just a model. I can guarantee that I would be writing this chapter differently in just a hundred years from now, if not sooner.

What this model suggests happened next was that more complex life forms adventured from the bottom of the ocean and toward the surface. As they did so, they 'experienced' a new type of clock. Near the surface, as the planet rotated, the light level they experienced would go up and down. Some life forms started beating to this clock and altered their biochemistry as a result.

The life in the sea regulated the atmosphere, so life on land could grab a foothold. The light of the sun regulated plant life from the get-go. When flowers blossomed, they opened to greet the morning sun and tracked it across the sky. The inclination of the Earth gave rise to the seasons and the cycles of growth and decay. Life on Earth followed the ticking of a clock.

Fish back then, as they do today, learned to spawn in time with another timepiece—they got in tune with the Moon.

The Moon orbiting the Earth and the Earth's rotation on its axis and its orbit around the Sun kept the clock beating for life on Earth for billions of years. As you will see, it still does, but we have largely forgotten about it.

At some point in the development of life on Earth, some of its inhabitants became self-aware. These humanoids became our ancestors. In passing, it's worth bearing in mind that it's more than likely that we are not the only self-aware lifeforms on the planet, and one day we might learn to 'talk' to dolphins and whales —and some species who might surprise us even more.

This amazing ability for some star dust to become self-aware only happened quite recently, some millions of years (or Sun orbits) ago, which is a blink in the cosmic clock of time. These self-aware lifeforms developed language and a set of sounds that correlated to physical objects and internal feelings and senses. The details of such proto-languages haven't been recorded, but we can imagine that they would have sounds for 'food', 'water', 'sun', 'moon', 'rain', 'happy', 'sad', 'hurt', and 'anger'.

By this time, such lifeforms were incredibly complex, and inside the bodies of these creatures (and us today) lay a myriad of clocks. These clocks governed cell birth and death; the clock of a heartbeat; a clock telling them that they were hungry; a change in biochemistry that informed them that they could procreate; a clock that told them when the time came to die.

In the same way that the nature of 'time' altered for the Universe as it evolved, our personal relationship with time changes over our lifetime. As for the Universe before First Light, pre-conception, the sperm and egg that we were made from have no concept of time. Everything just was.

When we are in the womb, for nine months or so, we have a relatively timeless existence. This is rather similar to the experience of time that the first stars would have had. For the first year or so after our birth, however, we might disrupt the time clocks of our parents while our biological clocks of needing to be fed and changed run riot.

Out from the Shadows

When we came down from the trees and became farmers, ways of counting time became essential to help us both plant and harvest at the optimum times. To count days and moon orbits proved easy. The inclination of the Earth gave rise to the illusion of constellations of stars coming and going from the night sky. Along with the position of the Sun in the sky, this allowed humankind to work with the seasons.

At some point, the need to measure time during the day must have arisen. Again, the Sun provided the answer. As any Girl Guide and Boy Scout should know (in my day at least), you can make a guess at the time of day by the position of the Sun in the sky. When it's directly overhead, it will be around midday.

Some enterprising earthling must have noticed that the length and angle of the shadow behind a tree could also be used to mark time. On cloudless days at least, humankind had its first clock.

People noticed that the moon phase changed over a fixed period, and from that, marked out time to 'moonths'.

Over the course of a year, they also noticed that the pattern and position of the stars at night would repeat across the seasons. This allowed certain predictions to be made about what was coming.

What is perhaps of more significance is that as this collective self-awareness of time grew, enslavement by time also developed.

Humans could count the years, which meant they knew how old people were. As a result, they could now predict how many years it might be until their demise.

People developed a sense that they'd better get a move on. The clock was ticking.

III : The Hands of Time

HUNTER-GATHERER SOCIETIES WERE PROBABLY THE FIRST TO DEVELOP A RELIANCE ON KNOWING WHAT THE TIME WAS.

Successful hunters knew that certain animals came out at certain times of the day, or night. Most of these time cues could be obtained by observing the Sun, the Moon, and the stars. Tribes would have a wise woman or wise man who became the go-to oracle on such matters. These days, we call these people Astrologers and Meteorologists.

As agriculture developed, synchronisation with the seasons made the difference between a healthy crop and a poor harvest. Because the goddesses and gods played such a big part, and some think they still do, it made sense to appease them at certain times of the year. Religions had feast days whose timings and observances were crucial, or so it was thought. As society developed trade and commerce, it became important to meet at markets on the right days of the month. It was from such societal needs that an agreed time system, which people could operate to, came about.

All Fingers and Thumbs

These days, we don't give a second thought as to why there are 60 seconds in a minute, 60 minutes in an hour, and 24 hours in each day. There is no particular reason our time intervals should be like this.

Our months, too, don't have to have different numbers of days in them, and we don't have to have 12 of them either. There is no real reason we must have 7-day weeks and 52.14 weeks in each year, with 52.29 weeks in a Leap Year.

It is, however, this system of time that we run our modern world to and the system that many of us rule our lives by. It works and isn't necessarily broken unless, of course, time pressures are placed upon us such that we feel stressed, over-worked, or 'fear-full' of the perceived lack of time.

Our current time system of 60 seconds, 60 minutes, and 24 hours is thought to date back thousands of years to the Sumerian culture. It is possible that it arises from cultures that predated them still further. Instead of our decimal counting system, they used what is known as base-sixty.

They used the phalanges on the forefingers of one hand to count to twelve, and the tips of their fingers on the other hand to count five sets of twelve up to sixty. It is perhaps no surprise that analogue clocks have faces, and time is read from their hands.

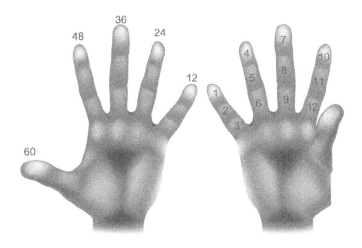

If the Sumerians had used the three phalanges on their thumbs too, we could have 75-second minutes and seconds, and 30 hour days. The Sumerians knew, though, that the number sixty had magical properties and could be divided by all the numbers from one through six. This is why we have half hours and quarter hours. The number sixty turned out to be useful when building complex and rugged architecture.

The time divisions of the Sumerians have been tinkered with by the ancient Greeks, the Romans, and more recently by the Church. In an attempt to back reference everything to the assumed birth date of Christ, in 1582 the Church even adjusted the whole calendar by a number of days. Indeed, this modern-day Gregorian calendar was named after Pope Gregory who instigated the change. Before that, the Julian calendar was named after a Roman emperor.

Our first five months are named after deities, and July and August are entitled in honour of Julius and

Augustus Caesar. The numerically derived month names of September, October, November, and December were the seventh, eighth, ninth, and tenth months. The reason for the unequal length of months is a little clouded in history but is perhaps an apocryphal rumour that the two Roman emperors had a hand in it by 'stealing' days from February.

Many cultures still use a thirteen-month calendar based on the moon phase. And in the West, some accounting systems are based on thirteen periods. In the French revolution, there was even an attempt to introduce a decimal clock with a ten-month calendar.

The system we use to measure time is now not only used on clocks but also to map the surface of our planet. We have 24 lines of longitude from which come our timezones. We can think of the Earth as a huge, rotating clock face divided into twenty-four time zones. No lines of longitude are visible from space when viewed by astronauts, who see a sunrise and sunset every 90 minutes. Incidentally, the use of these temporal divisions is relatively recent. The need for global harmonisation grew from an increase in international travel by steamship and cross-continental travel with the railways. The International Meridian Conference in 1884, instigated by Sir Sandford Fleming, adopted the international standard time system.

To run increasingly complex societies, humans developed clocks. These days, we use the vibration of caesium, and other atoms, to synchronise ourselves and our computer systems.

We only go to current accuracies of billionths of a second per year in our clocks through a long history of innovation and development.

Astronomical clocks such as Stonehenge were probably our first clocks, and primarily designed to mark time for mystical purposes. Note that, in the next few decades, when it comes to the subject of the ancient history of humanity, it is likely that we will be adding several thousands of years to the dates when sophisticated societies came about. Much was lost after the last major Ice Age.

In the pre-history that is accepted, obelisks constructed around 3500 BC in ancient Egypt are the earliest known examples of shadow clocks. The oldest known sundial is also from Egypt, dating back to around 1500 BC.

Perhaps so that we had clocks that worked at night or when it was cloudy, the passage of water from an upper to a lower container was used. The Ancient Greeks and Persians first developed these, and the Romans refined them.

The Chinese also developed water clocks, as well as using candle and incense clocks. All clocks like this had no external time reference, and would need calibrating. Amazingly, water clocks continued to be in use right up to the Middle Ages. Sometimes mercury replaced water for increased accuracy. Health and safety wouldn't allow this sort of clock these days.

At sea, the hour glass—which used sand—became the preferred timekeeping method, probably to help with shift changes of the crew.

Mechanical clocks began to be introduced in cathedrals and monasteries in the 13th century. In those days, they would be used primarily for calls to prayer. It was the introduction of the pendulum, which used gravity as a constant, and initially designed by Galileo, that took the accuracy of clocks up a notch or three. Galileo never designed an actual clock but, in 1656, Huygens used a pendulum to create a clock accurate to 10 seconds a day.

Only a few years after this, Huygens and Robert Hooke invented the balance spring, which led to the creation of a pocket watch in 1676 which was accurate to 10 minutes a day. We would be horrified these days if we had to rely on a timepiece with this accuracy. The latest Apple Watch, for example, is synchronised to within 50 milliseconds of Apple's own super accurate time servers. Our ancestors might be slightly baffled by our current obsession with time. Yet, despite all our sophisticated ability to measure time, currently down to an attosecond—one quintillionth of a second—many people complain that they are time poor and that there are just not enough hours in the day.

We now have clocks in every room, on our wrists, and on our phones, TVs, and computers, and we time our lives to some precision—whether it's catching a train on time, getting the kids to school, or sitting down to watch a favourite soap at just the right time.

The navigation systems in our cars use clocks in satellites that have been adjusted to take into account the effects of relativity, as they speed around the planet at 14,000 kilometres an hour, 22,000 kilometres above our heads.

These days, we take all of this for granted and are mostly oblivious of the real clocks that rule our lives and give us the sense of time passing us by.

Body Clocks

We can now plan our days to the minute with our electronic diaries, and run to tight schedules. We often ignore the clocks that really run our days. Although, currently, neuroscientists have not located a particular clock in our body that 'keeps time', our body is awash with 'clocks'. Their performance and functioning are what keeps us efficient, creative, and ultimately healthy.

Our cells must die and replenish themselves in time with their molecular clocks. If they don't, it can lead to a buildup of unwanted toxins and even cancers. Our heart runs to a beat. Our internal biochemistry tells us when we are thirsty and hungry. We know when it is time to sleep and when to awaken. If we get a bad night's sleep, or over or under-eat, it can take us a few days to get back to what we might think of as 'normal'.

These systems are, by and large, automatic. We can and do override them, perhaps by partying into the early hours or when the 'eating clocks' of babies run at different rates to ours.

The longest recorded time anyone has stayed awake is 11 days and 24 minutes. In 1964, Randy Gardner, a 16-year-old high school student in San Diego, California, intentionally stayed awake for 264.4 hours without using stimulants of any kind. After completing his record, Gardner slept 14 hours and 40 minutes and appeared to recover fully from his loss of sleep with no long-term psychological or physical effects.

When we do sleep, there seems to be a clock that tells us we are recharged and when to awaken. In teenagers, this clock can go a little haywire, no doubt as hormonal battles rage. It is worth noting that while we sleep time takes on a completely ethereal quality. For all intents and purposes, we are 'out of time'.

The Breath Clock

While some excellent research has been undertaken on biochemical and circadian clocks in our body and neurology, there is a fundamental clock in operation of which we are largely unaware. It is the clock of our breath.

The life expectancy of a giant tortoise is around 120 to 140 years, and an elephant lives for around 80 to 90 years. While our life expectancy is increasing, in the Western world at least, go back 150 years and it was between 50 and 60 years. Now here's the thing: A tortoise breathes around four times every minute. An elephant breathes around eight times every minute. And we breathe around twelve to fifteen times every minute. Tortoises, elephants, and humans all take around 400 million breaths in their lifetimes.

So, the first tip to changing our relationship with time is to breathe more slowly. A positive spin-off from breathing more slowly is thought to be that it increases our longevity. To learn to do this, we need to use our diaphragm and to do belly breaths. This, of course, is how a baby breathes. We've just got out of the habit as most of us breathe shallowly just using the intercostal muscles around our ribs.

Now, you don't have to do it all the time, but just doing 7 — 9 deep and slow breaths at the start of the day is enough to slow things down. You can also do it before any creative task or if you have been stressed. It works especially well if you are running late for a meeting. By breathing more slowly, we 'expand' time.

What's even more magical is that this technique works in groups, too, or when working one-to-one with clients. This technique costs nothing to try, and it's even possible that we can lose weight this way while also increasing our life expectancy.

When we speak, we normally vocalise on the out breath. The speed of breath gives rise to the speed at which we communicate. Such external communication is mirrored inside our heads in the form of 'self-talk'.

We don't often give this much of a thought, but the speed at which we talk to ourselves is around the speed that we talk out loud. The speed of thought, and talk, which is linked to the speed of our breath, gives rise to our sense of the passage of time.

So, it is only when we learn to talk that our personal time clock really begins to tick.

By using mindful meditative techniques, we 'un-learn' automatic 'self-talk' and retake control of our personal time machine. As you will see, it is from this meditative state that we are able to assume any time-full state we desire—be it past, present, or future. We are, after all, made of the same 'stuff' as the Universe, so we can learn to jump to any time state that has ever existed, or that exists.

Timeful Task : What Would You Do With More Time?

AS FOR MANY BOOKS, THE FIRST QUARTER OF THIS BOOK IS DESIGNED TO TICKLE YOUR TASTE BUDS, MUCH LIKE A STARTER BEFORE A MORE SUBSTANTIAL MAIN COURSE AND DELICIOUS DESSERT. THIS IS WHY TAKING A PAUSE BETWEEN 'COURSES' TO CARRY OUT A TIMEFUL TASK IS ADVISABLE.

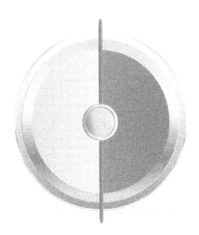

Let's imagine that time isn't quite as fixed or as finite as we think it is and that all the time we need is available.

Make a note of your thoughts on the following questions:

• What could you achieve, and what would you do, if you had all the time in the world?
• What would you like to happen more quickly?
• What would you like to happen more slowly?
• What would you do differently today if you knew you could take your foot off the pedal?
• What would you do differently today if you knew your dreams were just around the corner?

quarter 2

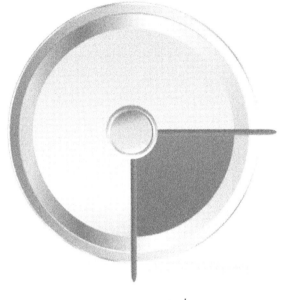

perceptions
of time

IV : Two Minds of Time

BEFORE GETTING INTO THE 'MEAT' OF THE BOOK —APOLOGIES TO VEGANS AND VEGETARIANS FOR THE METAPHOR—IT'S WORTH RECAPPING ON THE JOURNEY SO FAR.

To understand how to manage time mindfully, it helps if we think about how we have become so time poor in what is supposed to be a sophisticated and intelligent society. To help with this, we went back to the dawn of time to get an understanding of where our days, months, and years come from in the first place. We then looked at how humankind unwittingly enslaved themselves with time by creating a time system to allow our modern-day society to function.

We may not be able to control the rotation of the Earth on its axis and the speed of its orbit around the Sun. We might have little control over autonomous biological processes, like cell division, our hunger, and the need for sleep. When it comes to how our mind perceives time, however, and our overall efficiency and creativity, we have much room for manoeuvre.

The Divided Brain

Up until quite recently, most brain research was carried out on people who had experienced some sort of trauma to the brain. Neurologists could look at what function was impaired and map the corresponding part of the brain. So, a stroke victim might lose motor function, sight, or speech. Typically, this transpired on the opposite side of the body to where the brain trauma had occurred.

From pioneering research led by Professor Roger Sperry in the 1960s, the notion that our left and right brains had different functions came into our awareness. Amongst other findings, he discovered he could reduce some symptoms of epilepsy by severing the connecting structure, known as the corpus callosum, between the two hemispheres. Incidentally, he also undertook many non-invasive experiments, like blinkering alternate eyes from seeing what the opposite hand was doing.

As a result of this early research, the functions of our left and right brains became entrenched in popular psychology.

In many a Tom & Jerry cartoon you see a devil appearing on one shoulder and an angel on the other. A Google image search reveals that, commonly, the devil is perched on the left shoulder and the angel on the right. Erroneously, the urban myth took off that our left brain is logical, and the right brain is creative. Some people still espouse this like gospel, and sometimes even use it as an excuse, today.

It's worth noting that no other organ in the body exhibits such asymmetry where different sides undertake such different roles.

Today, advances in MRI and CAT scanning mean we don't have to cut brains open to see what has been damaged. Also, using chemical anaesthesia and radiation, neurologists can temporarily cause a part of the brain, or whole hemisphere, to cease to function, and ask a relatively healthy person what they are experiencing. What has emerged from this research is a completely different model for the brain.

The first thing to 'bear in mind' is that when people talk about brain asymmetry, and the left and right brain, it primarily applies only to the outer cortex. The limbic brain and the lower brain stem, or reptilian brain, exhibit less asymmetry. Secondly, even modern models for how the brain is divided are only generalisations. Our brains are known to be plastic and can rewire in an instant as we learn.

So, for example, some areas in the brains of Asian people, whose language uses pictograms, are wired differently from those who primarily use a symbolic alphabet, like the one in this book. If we to learn the other system of language representation, our brains rewire accordingly. Autistic savants and synesthetes, who might smell colours or feel words on a page, also have different wirings.

When it comes to changing our relationship with time, this plasticity and asymmetry becomes an asset. Such asymmetry is not confined to humans.

Some insight can be gained from the behaviour of birds pecking at seeds on the ground. It transpires that birds primarily use their right eye to look for individual grains to eat on the ground (whose images are processed by the left brain). Meanwhile, the right brain (fed by the left eye) is scanning for predators. So the bird's left brain is focused on the detail and 'the Now', and the right brain looks at the bigger picture, and what may be looming in its near future.

Kronos and Kairos

So, it transpires that our brain hemispheres have different relationships with attention and, as a result, time. In most people, the left brain pays attention to detail and largely processes learned behaviours and responses.

At the same time, the right brain looks for meaning and patterns and processes new information. The left brain sits in space and time, and the right brain is 'located' everywhere and 'everywhen' else.

As you read this book, your left brain will be processing individual words, while simultaneously, the right brain works out the overall context. If anything you read makes you stop and think, or confuses you, what happens is that both hemispheres have a little debate and discussion. It is remarkable that all of this can happen without us giving it a second thought.

While the right brain processes new information, when it is learnt and ingrained it gets passed to the left hemisphere of the brain to process.

Driving a car, or typing on a keyboard, being two classic examples. Try driving on the other side of the road or using a keyboard with a different layout, and you will get thrust back into that right-brained mode of learning. This could explain why it might seem to take longer to get to a new destination, but that time seems to pass by quicker on the return, or a repeat, journey.

While it may have taken advances in MRI scanners to work all of this out, the ancient Greeks might have intuited that we have two different experiences with time. They had two gods called Kronos and Kairos. The word chronometer is derived from the god Kronos, who looked after earthly affairs. While Kronos was busy on such detail, Kairos concerned himself with loftier matters by looking after the heavens.

Inhibiting the Inhibitor

It used to be thought that the butterfly-shaped structure at the centre of our brain, known as the corpus callosum, was the mechanism by which the two hemispheres inter-communicated. Nowadays, it is thought that its role is to inhibit one part of a hemisphere temporarily while the other processes something or other.

What follows next is descriptive and empirical only. So I have not tested this in a lab or had my head in an MRI scanner. I have, however, experienced both with myself and others, that when we 'inhibit the inhibitor', we can get both hemispheres to work together at the same time. When we do this, we enter an elevated state of consciousness called 'whole brain thinking'.

Not only do we increase our creativity when we are in this state, but also our perception of the linear passage of time changes and we seem to get more done with less of it. It is like 1+1=3.

A simple and effective way to keep our brain active is to exercise. This doesn't mean a strenuous workout at a gym. Just walking for 10 — 20 minutes a day is enough and, if you can, at a pace that gets you just short of being breathless. Walking not only increases heart rate but also blood flows to parts of your body and brain that it doesn't normally reach. I often go for a walk with clients, and it is amazing how a good walk frees up the most stubborn mental blocks.

What walking also does is move the cerebrospinal fluid that our brains float in. Incidentally, and almost literally, this fluid takes the weight off our minds using the principle that Archimedes uncovered all those years ago.

Cross Crawling

A specific type of walking, called cross crawling, seems to move it around even more, and increases the connection and communication between right and left hemispheres. Cross crawling is actually done best standing still, so you can do it in the office before embarking on a creative task.

It is important that you do it slowly.

1. Stand with your arms to the side and let the tension fall from your body. Feel the floor with your feet.

2. Now bend your right leg at the knee and swing your left arm in front of you and, if you can, touch your left elbow to your right knee. Or as close as you can manage at this stage.

3. Let your right leg fall gently and your left arm return and now bend your left leg at the knee and touch your right elbow to the left knee.

4. Try to repeat the exercise 5 — 10 times for each side.

If you find it difficult, or you seem to get your sides mixed up (like tapping your head and rubbing your stomach at the same time), don't worry. This just means your left and right hemispheres need this exercise. Either slow the movements down a lot or try it lying down. It will come in time.

Also, if you suffer from back pain or are otherwise infirm, just reaching for or touching your knee with the fingers of the opposite hand will be sufficient to induce the effect.

I first did this exercise over ten years ago, and after the exercise, I briefly started mirror writing. This is often a trait seen in those categorised with dyslexia. If it happens to you, take it as a sign that new pathways are opening up in your brain.

Mapping Your Mind

If you have ever been on an underground or subway system, without even thinking about it consciously, you navigated your way around using a map. If you were familiar with the subway, you would have been carrying the parts of the map that you needed in your head. And, if you are like me, this would even include details like which carriage to get on so you had to walk the least distance to the exit or interchange when you got off.

For an unfamiliar subway, you might carry a physical map or refer to one on the train or platform. What you may not have appreciated about this map is that it doesn't necessarily correspond to the actual layout of the tracks underground. That said, the colour coding and equidistant spacing of stations make it easy to grasp. Henry Beck created the London Underground map we use today back in 1933, and such is its usefulness, this has been copied by subway and overground systems around the world.

So, for example, imagine you had never been to Tokyo but I gave you a map with both Narita Airport and Akihabara circled. If I told you that Narita is where you will fly into, and Akihabara is where to buy the cheapest electronic goods, I reckon you could make your way there with ease and pick up a bargain—all without knowing a word of Japanese.

Maps are whole-brain devices that give the left brain the detail it needs while the right brain can see the whole picture. Accordingly, my tool of choice to get my left and right brain working together on the same task is the Mind Map. In my opinion, this is one of the best tools ever invented for creativity, learning, and memory retention. The Mind Map is the brain-child of Tony Buzan—quite literally the progeny that came from his brain. Incidentally, intentional use of hyphenation to concatenate and fragment words and phrases, like brain-child, is something that is incredibly useful for illumination and illustration.

Mind Maps are useful and elegantly simple devices. The reason they work so well is that they mirror the way the brain operates. The brain 'thinks' radially and by association—not in lists.

While there are many great software tools available on the market, the best way to be truly creative with Mind Maps is to hand-draw them. At least, that is, until the creation of the map is second nature and embedded such that using a computer doesn't interfere with your creative flow. The reason for this is that some people can end up in a left brained mode simply by engaging with a computer keyboard, screen, and mouse—or tablet. When we have a pen or pencil in our hands, not only do we use different neural pathways in our brains, but the map manifests into physical, as opposed to virtual, reality. This leads to a better chance of your creative project bearing fruit. On my creative writing workshops, computers are banned, even though I am a technophile. It also stops people taking sneak peeks at email and social media when they should be being creative—a sign procrastination is surfacing. If you do prefer to Mind Map on a computer, do print your maps out and stick them on a notice board or wall where you see them each day.

When it comes to whole-brain thinking, the impact of Mind Mapping is explosive in the amount of creativity it unleashes. Mind Maps are also beneficial for aiding memory, and brilliant for anyone studying and revising. If you have children, my advice is to get them Mind Mapping as early as possible.

In essence, Mind Maps are simple drawings or sketches of associations you hold between things in your mind. Normally, they start with a central topic, either in words or (even better) expressed as an image. You then draw branches from that image of the concepts that spawn from the central image.

So, if you Mind Mapped something relatively trivial like a shopping list, you might have a central image of a shopping trolley and branches such as fruit & veg, household, frozen food, beer & wine, dairy, and desserts. To make it even more memorable, you can use images of products on each branch.

What makes such a trivial Mind Map so powerful is that with a little training, you can forget to take the shopping list along, yet easily memorise all of its contents. I always Mind Map any talk I give on a single sheet of paper, and am then able to reproduce all the points I want to get across without any notes or slides. As an example, you will find a copy of the Mind Map I used to help me write this tome at the end of this book.

Where Mind Maps come into their own is in the area of creativity and especially free-flow brainstorming where previously hidden associations appear like magic.

The left brain is your navigator through life, and says to the right brain, 'Aha, a map! I like maps; leave this to me, I'll handle it.' While the left brain is thus kept busy, the right brain seizes the opportunity to sneak under the left's radar to unleash its full creativity.

Of course, this is a gross over-simplification, as our minds do not reside solely inside our heads. In order to really master time, we have to take time jumps outside and inside linear time and embrace the bizarre world of Whole Mind Time.

V : Whole Mind Time

IT TRANSPIRES THAT, IN MOST PEOPLE, OUR LEFT BRAIN SITS INSIDE TIME AND SPACE, AND THE RIGHT BRAIN SITS EVERYWHERE AND 'EVERYWHEN' ELSE.

So, if we admire a sunset or listen to our favourite symphony, our right brain will be primarily engaged. In these moments of awe, we become 'lost in time'. If, however, we are filling in our tax return, our left brain will be driving the bus. We might be worried about a looming repayment deadline and feel that time isn't on our side.

This temporal model for the left and right brain primarily refers to our sense of time in the outer cortex of the brain, where we process and run inner dialogue. It is thought that it is the billions of interconnected neurons in the cortex that give rise to our self-awareness. Underneath this outer cortex sits the limbic brain that we share with most mammals, where it is thought we process emotions. The brain stem, or reptilian brain, sits at the top of the spinal column and connects the outer cortex above with the rest of our neurology.

Current knowledge postulates that this area of the brain regulates autonomic processes such as our breathing and heartbeat. If true, there must be a clock or two 'ticking away' in our brain stem.

A model like this, though, where everything happens from the neck up, takes no account of the clocks and processes in the rest of our body. As there is a small time delay for signals to pass from neuron to neuron, intelligence and memory of how to operate must be distributed. So, the fingers of a classical pianist 'know' the music they are playing. This is known as 'muscle memory'. Neurons around our heart 'know' how to make it beat. The neurons around the intercostal muscles and our diaphragm 'know' how to operate our lungs. Of course, if we see approaching danger, inputs from our senses might make our heart beat faster and, as a result, make us breathe faster.

Decisions, Decisions

Some years ago, some neuroscientist noticed something strange happening with subjects in MRI scanners. If they were presented with a stimulus, like a flashing image, some of the neurons in the gut mind seemed to fire quite a few seconds before the stimulus was presented.

Our gut, or enteric mind, sits between the outer muscle wall in our colon and the inner digestive tract. In humans, the gut mind contains more neurons than a cat's brain. Although it may sound a bit bizarre, it transpires that we have areas in our neurology that work ahead of time.

This phenomenon is what gives rise to the super-sensibility of 'Near-field Precognition'. The field in question being the 'time field' we walk down. It is our gut-mind that 'knows' who is at the other end of the phone slightly before it rings. It also stops us pulling out at T-junctions and stepping off the pavement because it 'sees' oncoming danger before we are aware of it consciously.

The 'mind' that sits around our heart also has a different relationship with time. It 'knows' ahead of our conscious awareness if we will love, like, or loathe something. After an event, it also keeps signalling this state of 'lovingness' to our brain. 'Heart time' operates both ahead and after the 'now time'.

We can use the knowledge that our gut and heart mind possess awareness to save lots of time, especially when it comes to always making the right decisions. The signals from gut and heart minds are routed via the brain stem and processed by the limbic brain before our outer cortex becomes aware of them. As our outer cortex tends to 'speak' quite loudly, we can end up ignoring these signals and regretting our actions as a result. You will know what I mean if you have ever said, 'I wish I'd followed my gut,' or that your heart wasn't in it. To tap into the inner wisdom of our gut and heart mind just requires our conscious mind to instigate the dialogue, and to listen to and trust the response.

The first thing to bear in mind when eliciting such responses is that the gut and heart mind are old minds from an evolutionary perspective and don't possess language. Our gut will only give us a 'yes' or 'no' or a 'stop' or 'go' signal. Our heart 'speaks' in a level and so will be 'cold', 'lukewarm', 'hot', or 'positively boiling' about a situation it perceives. I mean the latter status in a good way, and not that you are fuming about something.

The second aspect of interrogation of our gut and heart mind is a little more temporally bizarre. When you ask a question, the answers come back slightly before we finish asking it. To experience what I mean, the next time you are faced with a decision, ask your gut mind first 'internally' for that 'yes' or 'no' and you will sense the answer coming back slightly faster than straight away. Incidentally, if you get a 'green light', go for it. If you are faced with a 'red light' from your gut, then you can either walk away or ask what would have to change in order to get a green light, and then ask a modified question.

The same sort of questioning works for the heart mind. If you get a 'hot' or 'boiling' response, go for it. If your heart is 'cold' or 'lukewarm', again you can ask what would have to change so your heart could fall in love with the idea.

If your head, heart, and gut are in alignment, you will rarely put a foot wrong. This is, of course, a massive time saver. By the way, I should emphasise that this procedure is entirely empirical. You can ask your gut and heart if what I suggest makes sense.

Out of Time

The observant among you might have spotted a possible error in the above analysis. When we ask our gut or heart what would have to change for it to concur with our head, if they do not possess language they might not be able to provide an answer. When you try this technique out, though, you will be amazed at the insights that you get from the procedure. To comprehend what might be going on, we need a more expansive model for both mind and time.

Just imagine a two-dimensional Flatland, with no concept of up. If we were to dip our hand in and pluck out one of its occupants, to other observers in Flatland, it would look like they'd disappeared. And similarly, a five-dimensional being would find it amusing that we are bound by our forward arrow of time. They would see not only us in the now, but all instances of us in the past, present, and future, all at the 'same time'.

Carl Jung, and many others before him and since, postulated that our minds are all connected via a collective consciousness. It has many names, such as the Cosmic Consciousness, the Akashic Field, the Noosphere, the Morphic Field, and the Super Consciousness. You will also find it called names like Satori and Brahman in theological and mystical literature. Some even refer to it as the Mind of God.

The idea behind the Super Consciousness is that all living, and non-living, things are connected in some way. Some physicists have theorised that this happens in higher dimensions.

The Super Consciousness is said to sit outside of our space and time, acting as a storage mechanism for all thoughts, feelings, wisdom, and knowledge.

If this is true, then the very thoughts you and I are having right now, are passing to and from the Super Consciousness. When we dream, we tap into it too. Every man, woman, child, animal, and plant that has ever lived is also tapped into it. This also includes versions of you and me in the future and the past. In terms of the you in the past, it could explain how we retrieve memories, or not. As for tapping into the you in the future, this would also explain so-called psychic phenomenon such as precognition.

As I mentioned, when you hyphenate words, you gain an alternative insight into their true meaning. For example, 'pre-science' and 'pre-cognition' indicate something that comes along before we get our science and knowledge. If you accept that the Super Consciousness stores all thoughts, this could explain how you can have an idea and don't act on it, only to see someone else coming out with your invention a year or so later. How annoying is that? It, perhaps, also explains how Leonardo Da Vinci had the prescience to come up with the ideas of both the helicopter and the parachute.

If you then extrapolate this idea of it further, there must be a version of you in the future who knows just what you need to do right now to evolve into being that person. When we interrogate our gut and heart minds, and they respond with a 'no' or a 'maybe', we can then ask what would have to change in order to get their sanction. When the answer comes back, it has percolated out of the Super Consciousness. An internal dialogue has stirred up an external 'conversation'.

While I stress that this is just a model, I find this process works every time I have used it on myself, and with others.

Moments of Light

So, tapping into 'whole mind time' is a great time saver when it comes to making a decision on a known issue or problem. Where tapping into the collective mind comes into its own is when we seek insight into something unknown. This could be an idea for a birthday present, the title for a book, or some insight into cutting-edge scientific research.

Such flashes of inspiration, known as light bulb, eureka, and aha moments, often arrive out of the blue, when we are perhaps least expecting them. When we experience one, we get the whole vision, fully formed, in what appears to be a fraction of a second. It was reported that Isaac Newton got the whole Theory of Gravity in this manner, and then it took him the whole of his life to 'do the maths' and write it all down.

People often get them while out walking or running. This is because they are inducing the whole brain state. People also get them when in the shower. The reason for this is that water is the conductor of the 'universal mind stuff'.

Entering into the meditative state is what sets up the perfect conditions for light bulb moments to occur, as a still mind gives space for new thoughts to arrive. This can be achieved with a 'formal' meditative session or during the natural points in the day when we fall into this state.

For now, what is of essence is an appreciation that such light bulb moments are not just whole brain events but whole mind events. When we experience one, all the mind centres in our body are illuminated by them. Our gut mind signals that it's a great idea, and our heart falls in love with it. Our right brain sees the whole vision while our left brain luxuriates in the detail. Our throat mind might even shout 'Eureka'.

From a temporal perspective, something more esoteric is afoot. Our minds and bodies exist in the now, experiencing our world, with a forward arrow of time. We have memories of what has gone before in what we call 'the past'. Light bulb moments are examples of 'future memories'.

I explore the specifics of tapping into such 'future memories' in the fourth quarter of this book, as they are examples of temporal alchemy. In the next chapter, we will explore how to enter the meditative state, at will, to allow them to arrive in the first place.

VI : Stretching Time

ABOUT ONE ORBIT OF THE EARTH AGO—THAT'S A YEAR TO YOU AND ME—I GOT INVITED TO PRESENT A MINI-WORKSHOP ENTITLED 'SLOWING DOWN IS THE NEW SPEEDING UP' TO AROUND 80 COACHES AND THERAPISTS.

The brief was to show them how to get more done in less time, both when working individually and in client sessions.

The first exercise I shared with them involved me taking them all through a light, relaxing and refreshing meditation. As part of this meditation, I stayed quiet for exactly 3 minutes and 33 seconds. When everyone opened their eyes and came back into the room, I asked them to make a note of how long they thought the silence had lasted. The ones that got the nearest got a prize.

Bearing in mind that the audience were all professional, intelligent people, the range of estimates were somewhat surprising. The lowest guess was around 2 minutes and the highest over 12 minutes, with the average being around 5 minutes or so.

Obviously, when it comes to matters of time, subjectivity plays a big factor.

It is this very subjectivity that provides the key for getting more done in what appears to be less linear time. If I had induced the meditative state with their eyes open in those who thought 3 minutes were around 12 minutes and given them a creative writing task to do, with a little practice, they could well have produced a higher output than those who thought only 2 minutes had elapsed.

Time quite literally is what we make it when it comes to our observance, and non-observance, of its passage. If you have been on holiday, have read all your books, and are waiting for a delayed plane departure, you will have experienced time seeming to stretch to eternity. So, when it comes to getting more done with less time, meditation is the key to unlocking this temporal door into a more productive, and creative, way to be.

One Thought at a Time

The normal human mind is only capable of experiencing one thought at a time. If we think about the content of a thought, we lose its direction. If we think about the direction of a thought, we lose its content. Just read those two sentences again and think about them to verify this for yourself.

Note, of course, that there is nothing normal about the human mind. As far as we know, it's the only bit of self-aware matter in the Universe. It's also capable of reprogramming itself in an instant.

Note too, that nothing about the mind is fixed, and even the singular nature of thought is not a given. A shaman taught me how to hold more than two thought streams simultaneously.

With this strange ability to only think one thought at a time, if our mind wanders away from the task we are focusing on, our efficiency will drop. This basic aspect of our consciousness leads us to the real reason we become inefficient. When our mind drifts, as it is prone and hardwired to do, our productivity drops accordingly.

Think about your thoughts during a typical day. Some of them will be mulling over past events. Perhaps you'll think about conversations that could have gone better. If someone crossed your boundaries, you could spend hours agonising about it. You might, of course, be harking back to pleasant times like an enjoyable meal, a fabulous holiday, or how you met the love of your life.

Alternatively, you may be planning and rehearsing a speech or conversation for a day or more ahead. You may be thinking of what to cook for supper, or longing for the weekend to arrive more quickly and for the working week to finish.

To add to all of this, there are all those pesky interruptions, diversions, and distractions. In an eight-hour working day, we are often lucky to get an hour of quality creative time. Note that being flexible about home working can help in this regard by giving people the space, and time, they need to operate more productively.

As a picture says a thousand words, this pie chart tells the story. The percentages, by the way, are approximate and as indicative as they are dynamic.

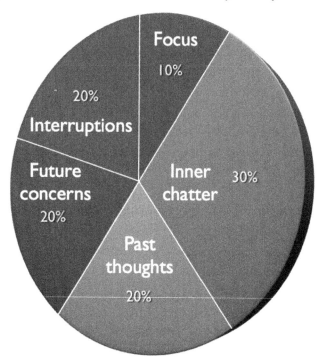

It is clear from this type of diagram that we could potentially have plenty of spare time capacity if only we could control the meanderings of our mind. With just a little practice, we can all bring our so-called 'monkey minds' under our control. When we learn to do this, our personal efficiency and creativity soars as a result. Such mind control is also made more difficult when we interact with others.

When we use these techniques in group meetings, exponential leaps in productivity are unleashed as a result.

It's Madness not to Meditate

Before I started meditating—over ten years ago—I thought there was no way I could make my mind go quiet. Also, being a busy guy, I didn't think I had ten or twenty minutes to waste each day. These days, when I do meditate daily, I have a much better day as a result and, as a result, I save the time back that I spent on meditation easily. Apart from saving the time back in spades, it's reckoned that for every minute you meditate, you even add a minute to your longevity. If true, it's a kind of madness not to give it a go and practice it regularly.

Meditation increases your vitality, reduces stress, improves your health and overall wellbeing, and generates aha moments just when you need them. Meditation isn't about sitting in a dark cave, chanting 'Om'. Rather, it's about taking some 'me time' every day. So, a ten or twenty-minute walk in nature has about the same effect.

You can also try daydreaming and enjoying a siesta, as did Salvador Dali. After lunch, he would put a spoon underneath his elbow, and when he dozed off, the spoon would fall and clatter to the floor and wake him up. He would then paint whatever was on his mind at that point, in that cusp between being awake and being asleep.

If you don't fancy sitting alone meditating, you can find a meditation group or take up something more formal like Tai Chi, Qi Gong, or Yoga.

Just learning to paint or draw, or learning to play an instrument or writing a book, are all great ways to experience the natural meditative state.

There are many types of meditation, but they fall loosely into two camps:

The first is known as Samatha meditation, and that is where you meditate on a thing, like a candle or a sound (such as a mantra) or—typically—the breath. As the normal human mind can only experience one thought at a time, when we think about something else other than what we're thinking about, our mind eventually gets to a lovely 'blank' state.

One of the great benefits of meditating on the breath is that the breath powers inspiration. When you think about it, inspiration is half of the respiration process. Typically, our in breath is when we inspire and when we are inspired. The out breath carries our aspirations to the world.

The second type of meditation gets you into a much deeper state. It is generally referred to as Vipassana meditation, where we meditate on thought itself. As we can only have one thought at a time, when we meditate on our thought, that thought collapses. As a result, we then get an instant connection to the collective consciousness that some would call our muse. At the same time, time itself takes on a different quality and stretches.

When it comes to 'learning' meditation, there are so many options open these days.

Mindfulness has become the new buzzword, and mindfulness courses can be found pretty much everywhere—either by way of meeting up physically or taking an online course. There are loads of apps for smartphones and tablets too.

Creating an Interruption Barrier

After a little practice, it becomes possible to enter a deep meditative state with our eyes open. When we do this, our thoughts take on a profile where our attention becomes primarily focussed on the task at hand. This is sometimes called 'entering the zone'. When we enter this zone, our thought processes look more like this.

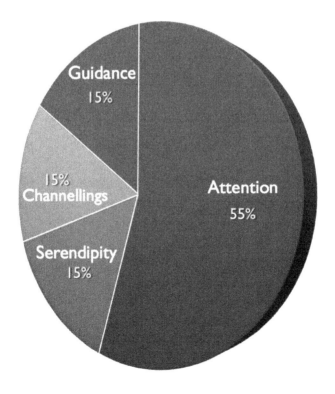

If any other thoughts do come along when we are in this zone state, they are often pointers and guidance that can help us better complete our task. When we enter this singular mode of thought, something else more magical occurs.

If someone ever comes to your mind when you weren't necessarily thinking of them, in all probability they were thinking of you at that time. I am sure you will have called someone at some time only for them to tell you they were thinking of you at that time. When we enter the meditative state with our eyes open, and we quieten our internal dialogue, we are not radiating our self-talk out to the collective. As a result, people simply don't 'think' to call and interrupt us.

I have lost count of the time that my phone rings just a few minutes after I finish writing a chapter.

Moving Consciousness

We don't give much thought to where our thoughts lie and where the 'we' that is thinking resides. Most people will assume that 'we' are somewhere in our heads, perhaps 'sitting' behind our eyes observing the world around us.

If we fall asleep, or faint, then this 'we' takes a temporary holiday while our lower brain stem, and distributed neurology, autonomously keeps us alive. When we awaken, or come back to our senses, this 'we' takes over the helm again and resumes 'steering the ship'.

As this awakened version of us largely inhabits the outer cortex of our brain, when we are awake, without thinking about it, we jump back into this world with 24 hour days and 365.25 day-long years. I suspect that, if we teleported to Mars, the Moon, or the International Space Station, we'd experience a time shift that makes transatlantic jet lag pale into insignificance.

When we enter the meditative state, as experienced by the attendees in my workshop, we jump out of time. We can use this phenomenon to stretch time, for sure, but we can also perform temporal tricks of an entirely different nature.

There is a meditative technique known as the 'Taoist drop'. It starts by closing your eyes and putting your tongue to the roof of your mouth, and then imagining a point about an inch up and two inches back. This is the top of our brain stem and the location of the pineal gland. From there, you imagine you are observing the back of your eyeballs.

What happens when we do this in meditation is that we can enter left brain and right brain time at the same time.

When your consciousness relocates to the pineal gland, it then becomes mobile. With a little practice, we can move it to the other mind centres in our body. We can move it down to our gut, and when we do this, we move 'ahead' of time into precogniscent space. We can move it to our back, which is a calm and serene place to be. We can move it into our root, which operates at a slower pace completely.

We can also move it through our crown and out past the top of our head, and from there access the collective consciousness. As you will see later, this opens up the potential for us to tap into 'future memories' and also access all states in the Universe, going right back in time to when it was created.

In this state of consciousness, we jump out of time completely and become a channel.

Timeful Task : Your Time Audit

BEFORE WE EMBARK ON THE NEXT QUARTER, IT'S A GOOD IDEA TO WORK OUT HOW YOUR MIND IS CURRENTLY OCCUPIED AND HOW YOUR TIME IS SPENT AT THE MINUTE.

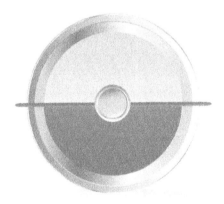

So, on two sheets of paper, draw two large circles. On one sheet, divide the circle into wedges, of proportionate size, of a pie that represents how your time is used up in a typical 'working' day. Label the segments with the types of tasks that take up your time. Note that the type of tasks, and length of day, will vary if you are a busy mum, an overworked doctor, or a student, for example.

On the other sheet, draw the segments of the pie to represent how you would like your ideal day to pan out. Note that you can do a combined chart for work and personal time, or split them as you feel. You could do separate charts, too, for the working week and your weekends. Stick them on a wall somewhere you will see them each day. By way of example, here's my perfect 'working' day, noting that as I largely love what I do these days, I can hardly call it 'work'.

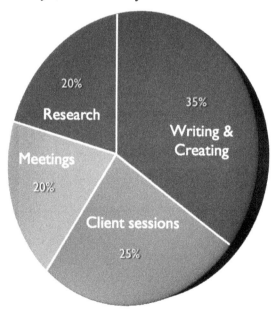

quarter 3

managing time

VII : Me Time

You will have picked up by now that I am a big advocate of investing in at least 10 minutes of 'me time' each and every day.

Perhaps counterintuitively, when we do this, it seems we get this time back several times over by having a better day all round. With less 'noise' going around in our heads, it also leaves space for us to notice serendipities that can help us on our way.

There is another, more subtle form of 'me time', which is this: Although we live, with over 7 billion other people, on a spaceship called Earth, which ticks along with its own days and years, we can change our personal time clock.

By changing the speed and nature of our thoughts and our perspective and attitude to time, we can dictate how fast or slow time passes for us personally.

This form of 'me time' involves us being engaged in 'The Now' where we are totally focussed on the task at hand.

By quietening the mind, we annul thoughts from the past and musings about the future and increase our productivity. With both brain hemispheres fully engaged, time stretches.

Lack of time, though, is one of the most useful excuses we can have for not getting things done. I have lost count of the 'times' when people have told me that they didn't have enough 'time' to invest in any of my mindful 'time' management programmes. They tell me that it's not the money at all but that they are time poor. Somewhat ironically, most time management courses deliver the time we invest in them back to us several times over.

One of the possible reasons that people hold such an aversion to learning how to better manage their time is that they may no longer be able to use the perceived lack of time as an excuse. It is said that we all have 86400 seconds to utilise every day. Assuming we sleep for seven to eight hours each day, this only leaves around 60,000 waking seconds, or so, for us to get things done.

Spending Time

The key to creating more hours in each waking day lies in becoming mindful about how we spend our time. By the way, I am not some sort of productivity guru cracking a whip to get everyone working at 300% efficiency. My personal mantra is 'slow down to speed up'. Personally, I like to get more done in less time, and with more ease, to generate more time to relax and enjoy myself.

The last timeful task was mindfully designed to give visibility to how we currently spend our time and to how we'd like to spend it in an ideal world. The concept of spending time forms a correlation with time as being a resource similar to money. With money, though, it is possible to generate more and more of it. Time, however, is seen as limited, linear, and finite. When we practice mindfulness meditation regularly, we find that time stretches and that it distorts in a non-linear fashion. Allocated tasks seem to get done in the time slots available.

With practice, we can stay in the meditative state with our eyes open and keep our internal dialogue to a minimum. When we combine this practice with the utilisation of both left and right hemispheres, at the same time, our productivity increases by at least 200%.

Investing Time

When we think of time as a resource like money, it leads to a new temporal possibility that, in turn, generates more time for us. The most successful entrepreneurs know the secret of valuing our time so that it creates more time for them.

For example, for the last ten years or so, I have invested around 35% of my 'working' time to create books and products that sell when I am asleep or when I am awake while otherwise occupied. Most of the books lead from one to another and as such create a volume of work that is larger than the individual components.

The meditations I record can be used to complement more than one book. They also save time for the people that listen to them.

After some cogitation either meditating or out walking the dogs, I will mind map each chapter of a book (or an audio meditation). It takes me between 2 — 3 hours to write 2000 — 3000 words and a similar amount of time to record and edit one of my meditations. As an asset, my spoken or written words then have the potential to bring in revenue, and hopefully to improve peoples' lives, for as long as our civilisation (and the Internet or something like it) exists.

Commercially, my aim is to generate a 'pension' that means I can enjoy my later years. I suspect and hope, however, that I will just continue to generate materials. Philanthropically, my aim is to create a legacy that helps others after I am gone. As I have no children, it's my aim that this legacy will be part charitable and part philosophical. It is said that there's only one thing you can take with you, and that's your evolution, and that there's only one thing you can leave behind, and that's your art.

Saving Time

While my aims might sound quite lofty, wise investment of time can be more practical and basic than that. For example, if you are cooking a casserole or a curry, it makes sense to double, or quadruple, the quantities of ingredients so that you have meals for the freezer that take less time to cook at a later date.

The richest people on the planet are also great outsourcers. They make enough money with their time that they can invest it in others who can make even more money for them again.

One of the biggest time savers is not having to do a task more than once. It takes time to pick up an unfinished task which increases the overall time it takes to complete it. When it comes to assessing whether a task is fully complete, we can engage in a dialogue with our gut and heart mind. This is a great way of keeping tabs on the efficacy of our output.

A more subtle time saver is the random act of kindness. When we bestow kindnesses on others, the world is kind back to us. This is a smart strategy, especially when our kindnesses take us a small amount of time for us to deliver.

Wasting Time

When we waste time mindfully, it's not a waste of time. As humans, we need to sleep and rest and recuperate. The point of life is not to work ourselves into the grave but to enjoy ourselves in what is a unique place, in our local cosmos at least. We get great benefit from our relaxation time when we are doing something that we enjoy with people we like to be with.

As humans, our spirit needs nourishment, so sitting and watching a glorious sunset would not be considered a waste of time. Time wasting is also subjective.

While I might consider it a waste of time to play computer games, a 'gamer' who makes $50,000 a month from demonstrating their prowess online to others would have a different perspective. I wouldn't waste my time seeing a boy or girl band in concert, but their fans might prefer a hole in their head rather than listening to Pink Floyd for a whole evening.

Being Creatively Uncreative

From time to time, we may spot that we, or others, seem to be incredibly busy and active but seem not actually to get anything done. We become creatively uncreative and procrastinate, finding loads of excuses to put off doing what we really should be doing. I have found myself acting like such a 'busy fool' on many occasions and discovered there are three common causes of this type of creative 'un-busy-ness'.

#1 : Fear

If the task that we are facing will cause us to take on board something new, it can cause us to be consciously or unconsciously fearful. We might be fearful that we get it wrong and that we might be ridiculed. It might take us to unknown waters. It might require us to step forward and be counted. It may lead us to success and magnificence. If you find yourself serving others before yourself, this is a good sign that a fear is lurking and in operation.

#2 : Framing

Sometimes we don't want to do something as we are uncomfortable about the task itself. It might be boring or something you wish someone else would do for you instead. A good example of this is completing a tax return. If we turn this on its head, the whole process of filing a return could be reframed as an exercise to let you know how much you can afford to spend on a holiday. You might have a dream holiday in mind for next year. In which case, you could see the amount of tax you have to pay as a measure of how much you have to earn to afford it.

#3 : Timing

If you are keen to get on with a task but external forces seem to get in your way, it might be because there is a better time to attempt what you are doing. In the next chapter, I explore how we can benefit from synchronising with natural time. In the meantime, if you feel you are pushing water uphill, the best thing to do is to sleep on it and see if you feel differently about the task in the morning.

Dream Time

While we have 60,000 or so seconds of waking time to utilise each day, there are also around 27,000 seconds of sleep time. It seems to be temporally balanced if I spend the remaining third of this chapter on 'me time' to explore how we can be creative while we sleep.

Our bodies need this time to recuperate, and it's part and parcel of being able to incarnate and survive in our physical world. Some mammals hibernate and take months out each and every year. My dogs doze and sleep for most of their days. I suppose we would if someone else was working to feed and look after us.

It is estimated that we dream for around half of the time that we sleep, so we have 13,000 or so seconds of dream time. How neat would it be if we could use that time to be creative? By using simple and repeatable techniques, we can seed, remember, and interpret our dreams. What's more, the quality of the inspiration we get in our dreams can lead us to enlightenment that is difficult to get to when we are awake, with our conscious mind active.

For example, apocryphally, Paul McCartney came up with the tune for 'Yesterday' in a dream. His dream was so vivid that he had to check he hadn't heard it somewhere else and copied it. More often, illuminations that occur in dreams come in an allegorical or metaphorical form. The German organic chemist Kekulé, while trying to work out the molecular structure for benzene—which he knew had six carbon and six hydrogen atoms—had a dream about a snake biting its tail, and subsequently discovered, or uncovered, the benzene ring, which became the basis for all organic chemistry.

When we are asleep, our unconscious mind is in full operation. It is keeping us alive, regulating our body temperature, beating our heart, and pumping air into our lungs—sometimes noisily when we snore. Our dreams are full of insight and illuminations that are normally suppressed or inaccessible to our conscious awareness. Occasionally, the dream may be literal and will not need to be analysed at all. If this happens to you, then great. When writing a chapter, or a blog, I often get the whole text in detail or sometimes as an image.

More often, though, the dream comes in veiled behind a layer of metaphor and allegory. For most of us, dreams come in images, although they can include sounds, colours, language, music, tastes, and smells. Numbers can be of special significance too.

The vividness of the dream is also worth making note of. The richer and more intense it is, the more you should pay attention to it. If the dream recurs, or the same theme is repeated, then there is undoubtedly a message for you embedded somewhere inside the dream. These messages can often convey information about our physical or mental health. They can even warn us about a situation we are in or about to enter that we have unconsciously noticed involves something we are uneasy about.

The cusp of being awake and asleep is known as the hypnagogic point. It is when our conscious mind is being put to rest. All we have to do to influence our dreams is write down on a scrap of paper, or Post It Note, the subject upon which we would like some insight. Pop this under your pillow before retiring so you will literally sleep on it. Don't worry if it gets crumpled, as you won't need it again. Then, as you drop off into hypnagogia, mull over the issue and especially what might happen if you get a positive outcome.

The perfect time to remember your dreams is between sleeping and waking, which is known as the hypnopompic point. The trick to remembering your dreams in the morning is to spend a little more time in the hypnopompic state. So all you have to do is to luxuriate a little longer in bed as you wake up, with a view to bringing the essential elements of the dream into your conscious awareness. All in all, it's a great way to start your day.

Then you write the bullet points only of the dream on your notepad, unless the dream is literal.

Once you've captured the essence of the dream, next comes the analysis phase. Apart from a bit of fun and research, it's not necessarily helpful to buy a book that contains someone else's interpretations of dreams. The imagery and metaphors of your dreams are always personal to you as they are seeded by your life experience. If I dream of an aeroplane, it might be because I associate them with holidays and not being in a metaphorical plane crash, for example.

In the first column, we have the bullet points of the dream. In the second column, write down what else they might mean to you. Then in the third column, list how the meanings in the second column might give insight and enlightenment to your situation. By making this two-level extrapolation from the bullet points of the dream, we bring it into a practical context.

What's so good about this method is that it costs nothing to try it. In addition, the practice of dream analysis can even have health benefits as it allows us to release feelings and emotions that might otherwise be bottled up. By far and away the best benefit is using time that is normally only used for sleeping in the creative process. You never know, your next million dollar invention might only be One Sleep away.

VIII : Natural Time

THE CALENDAR SYSTEM WE RUN OUR WORLD TO, AND OUR LIVES BY, IS MAN-MADE.

Let me state explicitly again–seconds, minutes, hours, weeks, and months do not exist in nature. We have made them up to help us run our society. By and large, they are a Good Thing unless, of course, we become enslaved by them or find ourselves watching the tickings of the clock.

Our modern world beats to a clock known as Coordinated Universal Time, which is abbreviated as UTC. Perhaps CUT didn't 'cut' it and sound temporal enough?

It is the primary time standard by which the world regulates clocks and time. It is accurate to within about a second and is, of course, only 'universal' as far as planet Earth is concerned.

At the same time, our years are now counted in accordance with the Gregorian calendar and referenced back to the birth of Christ.

This counting system, by the way, was superimposed years after the event and has been somewhat of a variable feast down the ages. These days, BC or Before Christ, has been secularised to BCE or Before the Common Era. The Common Era, or CE, has replaced AD, or Anno Domini. So, 2015 CE corresponds to AD 2015, and 2015 BCE corresponds to 2015 BC.

The modern world uses the Gregorian calendar, and UTC, to synchronise commerce, telecommunications, and transportation. From a spiritual and social perspective, many people use an entirely different calendar.

The Islamic calendar is a lunar calendar consisting of 12 months in a year of 354 days in length. It is used to date events for Muslims to determine the proper days on which to observe the annual fasting, to attend Hajj, and to celebrate other Islamic holidays and festivals. The first year was the Islamic year beginning in AD 622, during which the emigration of Muhammad from Mecca to Medina, the Hijra, occurred. At the time of writing this book, the current Islamic year is 1437 AH. In the Gregorian calendar, 1437 AH runs from approximately 14 October 2015 to 2 October 2016.

The Jewish calendar is also a lunisolar calendar, and the current Hebrew year is 5776.

The Chinese use a lunisolar calendar too, which is constantly adjusted with varying month lengths, in accordance with the Earth's rotation around the sun. The calendar is used to time public holidays and, privately, people use it to choose weddings and funeral dates and to select special days on which to launch new ventures.

Now, the population of China is around 1.4 billion people, and there are around 1.6 million followers of the Islamic faith. This means at least 3 billion people use one calendar to coordinate their lives with 4 billion others, and another calendar for a completely different purpose.

Extended Me Time (EMT)

The concept of 'me time' applies to each and every moment. When we enter the eyes-open meditative state, and have both brain hemispheres in operation, time stretches.

When it comes to planning and project management, we can use a calendar of our own making to go with the temporal flow and get back in touch with Natural Time.

It starts with the practice of being mindful of how you spend each and every day. If you are a morning lark, be creative first thing, as I am right now (or is that write now?). If you are a night owl, schedule your creative moments for later in the day or evenings, as do many musicians and performers.

EMT comes into its own when we use it to plan how we spend our weeks, our 'moonths', the seasons, and our years. When we have a temporal plan laid out in front of us, two things happen.

Firstly, it helps us focus on activities in 'the Now' that will help us glide smoothly down this path. Secondly, the future has a tendency to come along to meet us, with external events occurring just in the perfect time.

Magical Weeks

The names of the days of the week are steeped in mythology. They are largely based on the names of goddesses and gods of old. So, for example, Monday is the Moon Day and named in honour of the Assyrian goddess Selene, and Thursday is Thor's Day.

Without thinking about it, we ascribe attributes to different days of the week. So Mondays fill many with dread, and people 'thank their god it's Friday'. Weekends pass by all too quickly with Saturdays being sporting days and Sundays being days of rest or worship. Note, of course, many cultures have Fridays as a 'weekend' and work for six days. Other countries, like Sweden, are experimenting with 6-hour working days and how this improves well-being at a national level.

The days of the week are quite literally moveable feasts, and we can ascribe different tasks to each day to suit ourselves. Here's how my 'working' weeks pan out these days:

Mends Day : each Monday, I am mindful to mend and repair things that need attention in my life and world— and in helping clients.

Tools Day : Tuesday is the day I invest in building new transformative tools.

Weeds Day : Wednesday is a client day where I run unblocking sessions to weed out those internal gremlins that stop us being magnificent.

Surge Day : Thursday is my day to spend on marketing and pushing forward.

Free Day : Friday is my treat. It's the day I leave open for new possibilities to pop in.

Sitter Day : Saturday and Sunday are somewhat transposable, but this is generally the time to sit around, relax and socialise.

Sunny Day : again this might happen on Sitter Day, but being outside doing the gardening or walking the dogs is a big component of the week. To dogs, of course, every day is a sunny day, a sitter day, and a free day. Perhaps they know something we don't.

These days are not hard and fast, but I stick to them most of the time, and it seems to help me spin all my plates at the same time.

Mindful Moonths

Many vintners and farmers have twigged that the Moon has a significant effect on their crops. Sailors are respectful of the Moon phase, as their lives might depend on the height and power of the tide.

Astrologers are somewhat derided by their observance of the Moon phase and the position of the stars. One day, astrologers and astronomers will compare notes and find there is more common ground than they thought.

The Moon is the closest astronomical object to us, yet if you asked most people, they couldn't tell you the current Moon phase—never mind its distance from the Earth and in which direction it was moving relative to them. It's almost too much in our faces.

I discovered a few years ago that when I synchronised my projects with the Moon Phase, everything flowed with much more ease. This seems to work equally well for creative projects and marketing initiatives. I also found that workshops timed for the New and Full Moon filled more easily, and that book launches on the New Moon seem to be particularly successful. This book and its companions in the series follow this pattern intentionally.

The first step to tuning into Moon time is to work out where you are in the cycle. On a cloudless night, this is relatively easy, so long as it's not a New Moon. The quarter Moons can often be seen in the daytime, early morning, and late afternoon. Alternatively, there are loads of free apps for smartphones and tablets that give the Moon phase, or a quick search online will tell you straight away where you are in the cycle. Talking of cycles, the Moon phase is something that women are more naturally attuned to than men.

Once you know where the Moon is in its cycle, plan between the New Moon and Full Moon and act and deliver between Full Moon and New Moon.

Then, for projects that take around a month to work on, you can use the four moon phases to modulate your activity.

- New Moon to 1st Quarter : let the ideas percolate in
- 1st Quarter to Full Moon : dream of where the ideas might take you
- Full Moon to 2nd Quarter : evaluate and test the ideas
- 2nd Quarter to New Moon : take some action to make them happen

Note that there are two reasons why this works. Either the Moon is having an effect on our consciousness or it's acting as a big reminder in the sky that we should work through our concepts in a logical manner. If it works, it's academic whether it's either or both of these in operation.

A Plan for All Seasons

As the Earth is tilted on its axis by around 23 degrees, we go through seasons where the amount of day and night varies along with the weather. Only after writing three books did I notice that I'd started them all in Spring. Springing forward and falling back is the way I now manage my years.

So, every Spring there will be a major new initiative leading to a new harvest at the end of Summer. I use the Autumn and Winter seasons to research and plan what will be unleashed at the start of the next Spring. If you are someone who pays attention to detail, as am I, you can use the dates of the Spring and Autumn equinoxes and the Winter and Summer solstices to launch various activities. Again, these are easy to ascertain with a quick Internet search.

Now, if this all sounds a bit pagan, perhaps our ancestors knew of a simpler way to run their lives. Unlike our ancestors, we don't have to buy into any superstitions or dogma, but just to roll with the seasons. Like many of the techniques in this book, it costs nothing to try, and there's an upside to being mindful of all of our planning and timing.

Rolling with the Years

Once we get past the ages of 16, 18, and 21, we tend to celebrate round number birthdays like our 30th, 50th, and 100th. It's a wonderful thing to celebrate and reflect on our achievements and experiences of each decade. From a planning perspective, the seven-year cycle has certain advantages. Some of the reasons for this are a little beyond the scope of this book, but it's worth looking back at your life to see how the seven-year cycle is quite natural.

From when we are born up to the age of 7, our consciousness forms along with our sense of self-awareness. Between the ages of 7 — 14, our personality develops, and we begin to get an inkling of our place in the world. By the age of 21, we have fully densified into the physical plane, and our life pattern is set. It is how we feel about our lot at this point that dictates how smooth our life will be. It also determines what will happen over the coming seven-year cycles.

Some people will settle down and start a family. Others will travel the world. While some people are trapped at home. In many cases, there will be transitions and awakenings at the cusps of 28, 35, and 42. The mid-life crisis looms as we begin to realise we are not immortal. It can cause marital disharmony when children flee the nest. Some will question the point of everything when the realisation hits that the mortgage might never get paid off. When we pass 49 and 56, thoughts of retirement planning cut in, and from 63 onwards, some will be counting down the years.

The very thought of the cycles of life might lead some to depression and wondering what the point of everything might be. If, however, you are coming up to a seven-year cusp, a fabulous opportunity looms. We can slough our old skin, like a snake, and imagine where we would like to be in seven year's time. When we do this, we can make sense of all the previous cycles and see them as preparation and learning for what is about to unfold.

There is something less ominous about musing on the next seven years, as opposed to the next decade. The thought of how we will be in another ten years might be somewhat depressing and remote. A target of seven years from now is imaginable, achievable, and realistic, and can be filled with optimism.

Go with the flow.

IX : Just in Time

WHEN I WORKED AT THE BBC, MAINTAINING TV
CAMERAS, I DIAGNOSED A FAULT THAT NEEDED A
FAIRLY OBSCURE PART TO FIX IT.

I went to the storekeeper, found that he had one in
stock, and I requisitioned it. He refused to let me have
it because it would leave him with no stock, which he
said would leave him short in the case of emergency. I
tried in vain to explain that only three working
cameras in a four-camera studio was an emergency. By
the way, this storekeeper used to delight in saying, 'I
am a store-keeper, not a store-giver'.

As it happened, I engineered my way around my
predicament by designing a small circuit, using readily
available components, to emulate the part's behaviour.
Much to my supervisor's pleasure, this meant we
would never run out of stock again. I had used a bit of
time to create our own spares to save time in the
future.

The kind of stock-keeping in place at the BBC at that
time had its place when there was little visibility of

where the stock was coming from. In these connected and computerised days, manufacturers run Just in Time, or lean, systems where parts turn up just when you need them. This reduces the cost of stock holding and the size of warehouses, and probably the need for so many store-keepers.

When we become practised at running Extended Me Time (EMT), and being 'in the zone', we lose the fear of not having enough time, and the stress this brings along with it. We don't have to factor slack into our schedule, or to hold any stock of spare time back for a rainy day. When we run our lives to the EMT standard, something rather magical unfolds in the world around us. External events seem to happen in both the perfect time and when we are least expecting them. People who can help us on our path, show up when we need them. Enough money finds its way to us just when we need it. Enlightenments and revelations show themselves to us before we realise their real significance.

On the surface, this might sound like a naive and falsely optimistic way to be. When you experience it happening to you, as most people have at some time or other, it is transformative. Like all new ways to be, it takes a little trust and practice. You will experience false dawns and, if you are like me, can get over-excited by the early wins. The dividends to be earned are amazing and, like any investment portfolio, it pays to repeat and re-invest in what works well.

While we can be blessed by this approach to life, it also appears that we can be tested in exactly the areas where we can most benefit from the transformation and learning that such tests bring our way. It pays dividends, therefore, to be prepared for when the wheels come off the bus and life throws us a curved ball.

Dealing with Curved Balls

You may find it is relatively easy to run along to EMT when you are by yourself, but when you meet with others, their time clocks might be running at different rates, which can throw yours out of kilter.

Employers, fellow workers, family members, kids, and even pets have temporal needs of their own that can throw you out of your extended time perspective into a more phrenetic world. If this happens, there are some simple techniques you can employ to minimise the disruption. They take a little practice, discipline, and trust, and require you to be 'insight-full' about what happens when you encounter such interruptions.

The first aspect of being thrown out of EMT is to realise that your train of thought has been disrupted. Where you had been 'in the zone', your internal dialogue has taken a new course, which incorporates someone else's world. If the disruption is severe, it might stir up thought forms of anger, despair, fear, or hurt from your lower mind centres, and any thought of creativity flies out of the window. You can enter a 'mindfall' of someone else's making.

When this happens, and you feel events need your immediate attention, and before you dive into an alternate time frame, take three deep in and out breaths. If nothing else, this will steel you for what is about to unfold. If you find you have to drop everything, wrap up what you are doing and be thankful for the interruption, as it might be a blessing in disguise. Note that as I wrote this paragraph, a courier came to the door, and I came back to it realising this chapter needed a preamble and pre-frame. Before coming back to writing, I made myself a cup of tea and asked my gut was something missing, and the story about the BBC store-keeper came to my mind. This is something I had completely forgotten about until then.

If the interruption is severe, say like a family illness or a problem in business that diverts production resources, there may also be an underlying message. Something may need to be fixed in the business so that a bigger problem doesn't appear down the line. The illness could be a cry for help and an early warning of something that could be more severe.

If you find it difficult to unearth the underlying message, the Universe may be throwing a curved ball your way just to see what happens when you deal with it. In all adversity lies opportunity.

An Attitude of Gratitude

If you were to record all the thoughts in your head over a particular day and listen back to them, it might prove to be quite an excruciating exercise. You'd hear yourself commenting on people and events that you come across, rehearsing things you plan to say and conversations you have had. You might have random and creative thoughts. Almost certainly in the mix will be some thoughts of worry, fear, and perhaps even anger.

Our conscious mind only holds one thought at a time. It selects that thought from millions, if not billions, of possible thought forms that can be instigated through external events that impinge on our senses, and impressions that percolate up from our lower mind centres. Other thought forms from the collective mind can also sneak their way in.

One analogy that is often used is that our conscious mind is like the rider on an elephant that represents our unconscious mind. For some of the time, the rider is able to steer the elephant, but if the elephant wants to wander off on its own, the rider will be helpless to stop it. I am sure, like me, you have experienced this happening.

If the rider is holding the fear of being out of control, the elephant will be uncontrollable. If the 'rider' is angry, they can find themselves on top of a raging bull of an elephant.

A great way to make the rider stronger, and the elephant more controllable, is to adopt the attitude of gratitude. If we awaken and hold the thought of gratitude in our heads for the duration of the day, it helps us to see everything that comes our way as just perfect, and arriving just when we need it.

We become grateful for both interruptions and those curved balls. The learnings we get from dealing with them constructively is character building. If you are a writer, an artist, or musician, you will find that life's woes represent the source material, and ideas pool, from which your creativity can spring forth. If you are a creative facing the odd blockage, or disconnection from your muse, you will find that an attitude of gratitude allows the most perfect ideas to pop along, just in time.

Signs and Serendipities

The real role of the rider on the elephant of our unconscious mind is to become the director, observer, and navigator. Our unconscious mind is our protector, and it keeps us not only alive but also works ahead of time and 'knows' where we are going. The intelligent rider merely reads the signs and notices the serendipity.

If the going gets tough and obstacles repeat themselves, the rider's ability to count comes in handy. If the same difficult situation is encountered more than three times, there is undoubtedly a better and easier way. If the rider notices 'white feathers' on their path, these are metaphorical signs that they are heading the right way, and that everything is arriving just in time. Sometimes you will see actual white feathers in front of you which some people take as a sign. Most of the time, the signs and serendipities that help us on our road come along in other forms.

Messages can arrive as aha moments or in dreams. We might get told to read a particular book, or to see a film, by two or more people. My trigger is when the third person recommends something to me. If you are unfortunate to be in a third unhealthy relationship, either in your personal or work life, it's a sign that it is high time you did something about it.

Our world is awash with signs that can help us 'steer the elephant'. They come in the form of patterns, numbers on clocks, and car number plates. We may see symbols that can guide us, or newspaper headlines or blogs with information that can help us on our way.

The key to spotting the ones that can help us the most is, again, to be in the eyes-open meditative state, with a quiet mind, as much as possible.

Ditching your To Do List

When we embark on any transformative path—like learning to allow everything to arrive just in time—at first, it can involve us having to deal with a few demons. When the things that are sent to test us get dealt with, there is light at the end of the tunnel. It involves switching from dreading the tasks on our To Do List and switching over to using a To Love List.

We can get somewhat overwhelmed with our To Do Lists. Some people have several of them that they just add to, so that they never get any shorter. As a result, like our email In Box, they can get bigger and bigger and become completely unmanageable and unwieldy.

Some people even spend so much time curating their To Do Lists that they end up not getting anything done. It is said that when we love the work we do, we'll never work as such again. So just imagine if everything on your To Do List was something you simply loved to do.

Here's how to create a To Love List. You'll need two blank sheets of paper. Label one sheet of paper a To Love List and one a To Don't List.

First, scan all the items on your To Do List, or lists, and transfer the ones you would rather not do over to the sheet labelled To Don't List. Cross them off your To Do List as you go. You should now be left with a To Do List with just the things you like doing. Next, in the order that you would love to do them first, transfer them to the blank sheet of paper labelled as your To Love List.

Now have a look at your To Don't List. It will probably have things on it that need doing, even if you don't like to do them. See which ones you can outsource or delegate to someone else. Then take action to pass them on. With the tasks you have left, have a think of how you could tackle them or what would have to change with them so you would love to do them. Then move them across to your To Love List. At this point, you should be able to rip up the old To Do List and bin the To Don't List.

The next step is easy: just tackle your To Love List from the top down. This way, you will only do the things you like doing the most in the order you'd love to do them. What's not to love about that?

Timeful Task : A Whole New Year

As we finish this quarter on managing your time, it's a good idea to take better control of your time moving forward. So, spend a little time musing on the concepts shared in the chapter on Natural Time.

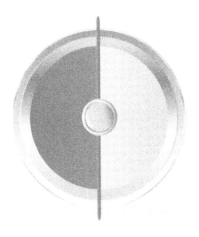

1. List the days of the week and put your own definitions on them based on how you would like your week to unfold (like I have with my Mends day, Tools day, etc.).

2. Find out the date of the next New Moon, and then list 13 things you would like to arrive, just in time, in the subsequent 13 Moon orbits. Put the list on a wall somewhere you will see it.

3. Find out the dates of the next two equinoxes and the next two solstices. Write down four things you would like to learn by the time they come around. Again, put this on a wall where you can see it.

quarter 4

temporal alchemy

X : Lives Passed

THIS LAST QUARTER OF THE BOOK IS SOMEWHAT OF A TEMPORAL POTPOURRI.

It consists of some loosely formed and connected musings on the nature of time. My hope is that you will pick up some scents that you like the 'smell' of and investigate them further.

It is unlikely you will find this kind of esoteric material in any other book on time management. You may, of course, think it is the rambling of someone who has lost his senses. Yet, everything mentioned here is something I have personally experienced. I have also met and spoken to many other people who have had similar temporal meanderings.

These three chapters come under the general heading of temporal alchemy, as they explore what happens when we manipulate and play with time.

Alchemy is the science and art of transmutation. Classically, the alchemists of old sought to transmute lead into gold.

They were, of course, forefathers of today's chemists and physicists who, with enough energy, can pull off that trick and can even form diamonds from graphite.

Up to now in this book, I have mainly explored how time can be elongated and stretched and how we can get more done with less of it. I feel I would be short-changing readers if, in this last quarter, I did not share what else I have experienced and discovered in my explorations in time.

In the three-dimensional world, we are easily able to manipulate objects and reorientate them in space. We can make the branch of a tree shorter and mould jelly into all kinds of ornate shapes. We are accustomed to thinking that time is un-malleable and finite; however, the temporal alchemist sees time as an infinite resource that can be tapped into at any point in time, played with, and even created.

So, as three-dimensional beings, we can easily manipulate two-dimensional shapes. For example, we can take a flat sheet of paper and curl it into a cylinder. If a Flatlander lived on that paper, they could now walk around their world and come back to where they started, without falling off two of the edges at least. This is rather like us circumnavigating the Earth.

Correspondingly, a five-dimensional, or higher, intelligence would find it easy to manipulate time, as well as space, in our world. It is said that we are not so much humans on a spiritual journey but spirits on a human journey.

This implies there are multidimensional beings having a three-dimensional experience. The dimension of time is thrown into the mix, so we don't experience everything at once. We are able to access our higher dimensionality from which we can access all times and all space. The key to doing this lies in entering the Extended Me Time state and extending it a little further.

Past Lives

By way of example, I discovered some years ago that the past is still accessible to us, and not just the recent past but all time that has passed.

I went on a past life regression course some years ago. I took the course for the purposes of research on a book I was writing, and not so I could become a practitioner of past life regression. Pretty much on the first day of the course, something weird happened. Spontaneously, I saw past and future versions of people in what can only be described as their aura. I have since discovered that virtually everyone can do this, and I've demonstrated it in mixed groups of around 50 people. Bizarrely, it also seems to work over Internet video calls.

Even though, these days, I can experience this phenomenon at the drop of a hat, I don't go around peering at people to see things I have not been given permission to see. I also have few past life memories of my own, other than what some mediums have told me. One weird memory did surface on the course, though.

When I got regressed, I didn't go back to the court of Henry VIII or imagine I'd built the pyramids. I got the strong sense I was a smooth, floating egg-shaped blob with dark patches where my arms and legs would have popped out. I sensed this was tens of millions of years ago in pre-history. I then sensed I was obliterated by a meteorite.

Some years later, I read a book called Cosmic Memory by Rudolph Steiner, and in it, he describes one of the early root-races of humanity as being exactly as I envisioned. A couple of years after this, while in a client session with a lady who was also adept at past life regression, I shared this story with her. Imagine my surprise, and you could not make this up, when she told me that on her past life regression course, she remembered being a meteorite that hit the Earth and obliterated life on the planet.

Re-incarnation

Since taking that course, I have ended up helping many people by using the regression techniques I learned. As the instructors on the course told me, it either works so well, and instantly and permanently, because we have actually had past lives, or because we imagine that we have. If it works, it is academic which holds true.

Whether you believe in reincarnation or not, past life regression seems to help us heal in 'the now'. Personally, I am open to whether we do reincarnate or not. If we do, I don't believe this version of 'Tom Evans' will ever come back but that an overarching essence, or soul imprint, carries on, both down and back up the timelines.

Our DNA may prove to be one of the mechanisms by which past life memories are carried from generation to generation. There is much so-called 'junk DNA', which could act as a 'tuning fork' that resonates across space and time with others that are similar to us. This could also explain why it appears that more than one person has a memory of a single historical character. Our DNA may not only dictate our features and susceptibility to certain diseases but also our talents and skills, as well as aspects of our personality. What we like and dislike and what we are like may resonate with what our ancestors were like.

Morphic Resonance

If you think about it, the part of the Universe we resonate with most strongly is the version of us, and all our atoms and molecules, that existed just a second ago. Going back in time, we also strongly resonate with the versions of us that existed an hour ago, a day ago, a month ago, and so on.

All living things are surrounded by a life field or aura. You can learn to feel it in minutes and to 'see' it with a little practice. When a creature or plant dies, the field leaves. It is a slight misconception that this field is somehow generated by the organic matter it envelops. A more accurate model is that the living being is distilled and crystallised by this field into what we call reality.

This field is described by the wonderfully maverick Rupert Sheldrake as the 'morphic field', which holds the 'pattern' for the being it creates. If a salamander loses and regrows its tail, it is thought that the morphic field contains the information that facilitates its regrowth. Incidentally, if the field is damaged or weakened, we get ill. Conversely, the practice of daily meditation and diaphragmatic breathing builds and strengthens our life field.

The morphic field contains the imprint of us from the past and holds our pattern, so we don't disassemble as a messy pool of goo on the floor. It also contains an imprint of all events that have passed in this life and, if you adhere to the model, those that occurred in past lives too. So any traumatic experiences can stay with us and limit our ability to shine and move forward.

For example, I was the cleverest boy in class in primary school and so was given the role of Joseph in the Nativity play, at about age seven. After the first rehearsal, it became clear that I couldn't act, as I was petrified, so I got demoted to the role of an innkeeper. I couldn't even say, 'There's no room at the inn,' so I ended up as an angel on the back row of the chorus without any wings. I think I just mouthed the words of the hymns. Rolling forward forty or so years, I would always play second fiddle in business presentations and felt similarly petrified if I became the centre of attention. It took a single regression session to remove this fear, which I discovered was actually seeded five lifetimes before this one, be they real or imaginary ones.

Time-based Therapy (TBT)

So where regression techniques really come into their own is in helping to remove stubborn procrastination, or nagging illnesses, that won't go away. Both, of course, have a significant impact on our productivity and efficiency in the present. Such regressions don't necessarily involve going back to past lives. Sometimes the debilitating issue is seeded in childhood, or even when in the womb.

It is my belief that when I 'see' past lives in peoples' auras, I am really peering into the morphic field. The reason I am led to think this is that I've been able to heal specific damaged parts of the body by seeing that part in the past when it was okay, and then by 'softening time', allowing the damaged part to be renewed, much like a salamander regrowing its tail. Note that when I use this healing technique, I make sure that the patient is very much a part of the temporal loop and also 'sees' the transformation and transmutation.

With this technique, I've removed rashes, healed damaged ligaments and even in one case repaired an internal part of the body that would only have been visible by X-ray or MRI. I should hasten to add, I don't bill myself as a healer and most of these cases have been when working with friends to see if I could help in parallel with conventional, allopathic treatment. The results seem to be 'out of this world', though.

Forgiving What's Passed

Another regression technique seems to work particularly well with dealing with psychological dis-ease. If we imagine that a character trait we possess 'in the now' was seeded in the past, we can deal with it by going back in time to when the dis-order surfaced. When we do this, remarkably the person in the present gets instant relief from whatever it is that troubles them.

In light hypnosis, or meditation, we send love, forgiveness, and gratitude to the version of us that experienced the trauma. We thank them for having suffered and gone through that experience just so we could be free of it now. Occasionally, we have to get that old version of us to send similar messages further back down the timelines to heal ancestors long passed.

Now, if this sounds bizarre and a flight of the imagination, let me concur—it is bizarre and imaginary. Yet, the relief that people can benefit from 'in the now' is immense. Regression is a good example of a 'talking therapy' that works particularly well. Occasionally, such mental trauma can lead to physical ailments such as allergies and food intolerances. In cases where I have come across such linkages, I have been amazed at how a multi-level healing takes place.

Of course, if you can send messages back to an earlier version of yourself, it is possible that a 'future version of you' is sending messages back to you right now.

Again, I stress that this is a flight of imagination. Yet, imagining that it is a possibility can lead to amazing flashes of enlightenment and inspiration.

By the way, in this book, the future is just one page turn away.

XI : Future Entanglement

EVERYTHING IN THE UNIVERSE SPINS IN SOME MANNER OR ANOTHER.

Our sun and billions of other stars spin on their axis and around the centre of our galaxy. The Earth spins around each day, and around the Sun every year. The elementary particles that our atoms are made of all spin too.

Quantum physicists have discovered something weird about spin. If you separate two particles that were once connected, when you subsequently alter the spin of one of them, the other mirrors the new spin. What's even stranger is that the information passes from one particle to the other faster than the speed of light. For faster-than-light travel to occur, the communication has to be in a higher dimension.

It is through such entanglement that the morphic field resonates across space and time. This same form of entanglement scales up so that we are entangled with both past and future versions of ourselves. Furthermore, and this might be a bit mind bending, so bear with me, when we send a message to the past or the future, it gets there instantaneously. So, changes we make in 'the Now' ripple up and down the timelines before we can say boo to a goose.

In the same way that we morphically resonate strongly with past versions of ourselves, we also resonate with the version of us a second from now in the future, a minute from now, several months from now, and so on. When I began to see past lives in the aura, I soon discovered that older and future versions of people were equally visible if I tuned into them.

It is said that the best way to predict the future is to create it. So, once we plant the seeds for the most perfect future to come our way, we can fully immerse ourselves in the here and now. Both our efficiency and enjoyment increase when we embrace the Now with gusto. I hope you can see now that this is how the last timeful task, where you mapped out the year ahead, sets things in motion.

You can extend this task and plan out where you would like to be in 7, 14, and 21 year's time. When we do this, and meditate upon it, a perfect version of us in the future picks up this message and entangles with us in the Now. When we then concentrate and focus on what we are doing right now, ideally that will help us get there, and we get pulled towards that future version of us.

I hope this hasn't tied you in too many temporal knots.

Opening to Channel

As I mentioned, it's conjectured that we are all connected by a universal field or collective consciousness. It is thought that this field contains all thought, be it past, present, or future. Others have postulated that this field envelops the planet in what is called an Akashic Field, an I-Field, or Noosphere. If such a field does exist, it will be in a higher dimension, so I feel it's somewhat limiting to locate it in space. I am sure that the astronauts and taikonauts who go to Mars will still be entangled with it and can connect with it.

As this field stores all thought, it holds our memories both in this life and, if this fits your model, in past lives too. As it sits outside space and time, it also contains all thoughts and knowledge that future versions of us have. When I am writing, and I stress this might be imaginary but it seems to work, what I do while in the EMT state is to tune into the future version of me who 'knows' the words I have yet to write. I am doing this now!

The first time I learned this could be possible was while writing a short story called Soulwave. For the plot, I wanted Mars and the Earth to be on opposite sides of the Sun sometime in the 22nd century. I plucked a date out, at random, and inserted a comment to go and check it later. I found an online solar system where I could wind the clock forward, and discovered that the two planets were exactly where I wanted them to be on the exact date I'd selected.

Now, of course, this could be chance, or a version of me could have been on a spaceship orbiting Mars on that date. A more plausible, yet admittedly weird, explanation was that I tapped into the version of me, a few days in the future, that had found the date from the online solar system.

I discovered, some time after this and other bizarre events had happened, that people refer to such wisdom gathering as channelling. What happens is that we get our conscious mind out of the way and tap into the collective.

Channelling my future self is my preferred method these days, but I have worked with authors and artists who channel the ascended masters, the angels and archangels, and the fairies down the bottom of the garden.

Some mediums channel the dear departed, and you can 'channel' animals, plants, mountains, and even the Moon, the planets, the Sun, and the stars.

Again, personally, I don't care if a real communication has been established or whether it's just an example of an over-active imagination.

All I know is that I receive a lot of information that I couldn't possibly know, and I seem to be able to write speedily and with confidence and clarity. I allow readers to judge whether or not I pull that off.

Messages in Time

Forging a connection between us in the Now and our future self, opens up another possibility for us that can both save time and allow information to get to us 'just in time'. As we are entangled with our future self, our future self can also send information to us in the Now.

Conversely, we can ask our future self for a message or a sign. If our mind is busy chattering away, however, we might not hear the message. When such messages arrive, we call them light bulb moments.

To imagine how this might work, you can send an imaginary message back to a past version of you right now. By way of example, let me share my earliest memory of experiencing an aha moment, which came —out of the blue—in a maths class. The teacher struggled to get the basics of algebra across to a bunch of twelve-year-olds. I'd picked up what he was trying to teach ages ago, so sat looking out of the window in a dreamy state, wishing he'd get on with things. He must have spotted me, and said, 'Evans, boy, do you get it?'

I replied that I did, so he held up his piece of chalk and asked me to come up and explain it. Although quite bright, I felt incredibly nervous about standing up in front of the class, much less at explaining algebra. Somewhere between leaving my desk and walking toward the blackboard, I had a vision. I drew a see-saw and put the algebraic terms on each side of it. As I moved things around, I showed how the see-saw could be made to balance and the equation be solved.

To this day, I don't think this kind of visual mathematics is taught in schools. More's the pity, as the whole class got it, and the teacher got off the hook.

I only came up with this memory while writing my book, New Magic for a New Era, where I also shared this anecdote. While writing that book, I had the idea that I ought to send see-saw allegory back to the 12-year-old version of me.

The Anatomy of a Light Bulb Moment

If your future you is trying to tell you something, clearly it could be important. How would you know if you received such a message, as opposed to any old kind of thought or whimsy?

Some time after I wrote my book on light bulb moments, it occurred to me that I should research what was known about what happens to our neurology when we receive such a message. My research drew a blank, so I decided to channel in the answer, and what I got in meditation came in as a light bulb moment. I got the whole vision in a flash. The following shows the result:

The fuel to encourage the reception of a light bulb moment is specifically delivered during the inspiration phase of breathing. As neurons do not have internal reserves for oxygen, more neuronal activity requires more oxygen to be delivered rapidly through the blood stream. Conventional wisdom suggests that more neuronal activity creates more connections, and the likelihood of a 'new' connection being forged increases as a result. So, deeper breathing while meditating causes more of this potential interconnectivity in the brain. This could also be why ideas come in while out running.

When we move our diaphragm, which is sometimes referred to as the spiritual muscle, it pump-primes your pranic tube, which is life force that stems from your spinal column. This in turn stimulates your main conglomerations of neurons, centred at the main chakra points, and a massive amount of intercommunication ensues. Initially, this is mainly between your gut, heart, and third eye.

After a few minutes, the pranic force seeps outside your physical body. There is a point known as your omega chakra, a few inches below the bottom of your spine—your root chakra point. From there, your prana seeps into Mother Earth and informs her you are ready to receive.

A nanosecond later, it rises up your spine, past your crown, to a point just above your head, known as the alpha chakra. At this time, you become the pivot point between the superconsciousness, connected to your future self, and Mother Earth—with your heart being at the very centre. Sometimes a big tingling up and down your spine can accompany this whole process.

If at that time you remain internally silent, the information transfer occurs. It seems to happen inside time and outside space. Every neuron in your brain lights up, and you experience the beginning of a light bulb moment. The process is not yet complete.

The information is passed to Mother Earth, who checks that it is safe and timely for you to receive it. She checks to see if the idea is ecologically sound for you, Her, and all beings on the planet.

Your root and sacral chakras are then consulted about the safety of the idea from a personal perspective. It next passes into your gut centre for further 'internal quality assurance'.

If your gut gives you a 'yes', your gut then passes it to your heart centre so you can fall in love with the idea. The heart mind communicates upwards with a sliding scale where a zero [or negative] representing the loathing of the idea and a ten [or eleven] that you are totally in love with it.

The idea then returns to your pineal gland at the top of your spinal column and the centre of your brain. From there, it permeates to enter your outer cortex and leaks into your consciousness. You then become consciously aware of the 'new idea'. It is first decoded and interpreted by the right hemisphere, which looks at it from a holistic perspective. Finally, it is passed to your left hemisphere for 'processing' of the detail.

In real time, much less than a second has elapsed. Yet, as all your 'minds' are in agreement, you know you have to act on this 'news'—it just feels right. When the light bulb moment percolates through our neurology fully, often our throat mind can't wait to tell the world about it.

Pebbles in the Pond

If this notion intrigues you, the way to initiate such communication is to drop some pebbles in the pond of the universal thought field.

First, ask questions to which you would like the answer. Then be open to receive the information.

Secondly, send answers back to younger versions of you to questions you now know the answers for. This works especially well if you think back to points in your life where you made choices between one direction or another. Just imagine that it was the future version of you nudging you in the right direction all along.

XII : Down the Rabbit Hole

IN THIS 'TWELFTH HOUR' OF THIS BOOK, I'VE COLLATED A SMORGASBORD OF TEMPORAL ANOMALIES TO PIQUE THE INTEREST OF FELLOW EXPLORERS.

I have spoken to a few people who have experienced some events that are similar, which gives me some comfort that I am not going mad.

Furthermore, in the majority of cases, I have not consciously induced these happenings or tried to reproduce them—they just happened, and I noticed them. As the conscious mind doesn't spot everything, I am sure they happen more frequently than we notice, and I would love to hear from readers who have experienced similar time 'slippages'.

I should also share that I am picking up from various 'channels' that it appears we are on the cusp of a dimensional shift, and such anomalies are signals that the reality we think of as 'reality' might be changing and moving up a gear or three. I should also state that no alcohol or drugs were involved with inducing any of these incidents.

I should also emphasise that I am not time-obsessed. I don't wear a watch but am rarely late for meetings or project delivery. I don't particularly watch movies or TV shows or read science fiction books on time travel.

Jumping Time

When I first learned to meditate, as I entered the trance state, I would often feel a light jolt at the back of my head, in the cerebellum. It wasn't uncomfortable or scary, but as though a shift in space and time had occurred.

One evening, some years ago, I was sitting in my living room alone reading a novel called 'Herstoria' by Wendy Salter, which explores the intertwining of past lives. The book's subject might have caused what was about to unfold, and I stress that no beer, wine, or spirits had crossed my lips. I turned a page and experienced that jolt at the back of my head, and jumped back in time by around ten minutes. I was still holding the book, but I'd gone back by quite a few pages. I thought there was nothing for it but to read them again and re-live those few minutes of my life.

Another strange event occurred a day before I was due to run a workshop called 'Bending Time'. I was driving to Gatwick Airport to pick up a lady who was assisting me to deliver the course. Again, I was not under the influence. As I drove east on the A25, approaching the town of Dorking, my mind drifted and wasn't thinking about anything in particular. As you enter the town of Dorking, you go into a one-way stretch lined with some enchanting antique shops. I saw none of this, but I do remember approaching the traffic lights before Dorking. The next thing I knew was that I was driving on the A25, still going east, but about two miles on the other side of the town. I had no memory of actually driving through the town centre. Both my car and I had jumped space and time in some way.

Neither type of incident has happened to me since, to my knowledge, but I remember both occasions vividly and I 'knew' at the time that something strange had just happened.

Moving Times

On a similar note, I should also share something that is perhaps tamer and that you can try yourself. A close neighbour in my village asked me at a party if any of my meditations would help with reducing jet lag. At the time, he was travelling to and from Brazil from the UK every week and spending all weekend sleeping. The result was that he saw little of his family.

I thought about it for a moment and remembered that a shaman mentioned a jet lag reduction trick to me. A few days ahead of your trip, you imagine that you send an aspect of your being, called the 'subtle body', on ahead of you. You then make the trip and your physical body, called in this context 'the gross body', catches up. You do the same trick when making the return journey.

So, before his next trip, I recorded a specific meditative visualisation for my neighbour, and he listened to it. I was as surprised as anyone when he told me that it worked perfectly in both directions. This visualisation, which is available from the Meditations page of my website, has since helped loads of people get from one side of the planet to another.

For those who are so interested, the same type of visualisation can be used for what is termed 'remote viewing'.

Stopping Time

I have had very little formal meditation training. I did, though, visit a lady some years ago to learn about a specific spinal breath technique. The sessions were pleasant and relaxing and basically involved me lying down and breathing. During what was about my third visit, I followed her gentle guidance, and after a little time I felt a little strange and mentioned this to her. She told me that she was not surprised as I'd just done a whole body levitation.

I didn't feel scared, and the feeling was that gravity and I had changed our relationship and temporarily disassociated from each other. I did think afterwards that it was handy that I was indoors. Not that I reached the ceiling, but levitating outside and not knowing how to 'un-levitate' could be somewhat dangerous as the sky would not necessarily be the limit.

I had a couple of sessions after this and, not that we tried to repeat the levitation, it turned out to be a one off. I should state that I think I know how to go about repeating the experience, but I don't feel minded or 'guided' to try. I did discover that when time stops, physicists think that strange things might happen to gravity and, perhaps, 'locally' that's what happened to me on that rainy, grey day in Woking.

I hadn't given this incident much thought, or even credence until just a couple of months ago when I interviewed a chap called Randy Rogers for my Zone Show podcast. He shared with me a similar levitation incidence he'd experienced when he was in a past life regression session. I am encouraged that I'm not going mad, and that other people have had similar experiences. This podcast interview reminded me of another levitation experience from history.

The Dominican philosopher and theologian, Thomas Aquinas, was rumoured to have been observed levitating when deep in prayer. Now that I mention that, even though I seem able to 'see' past lives, I don't have many past life memories. It is perhaps just a coincidence then that I was three weeks late out of the womb, born on Thomas Aquinas' feast day, and my parents named me after him.

Rejuvenation

This particular technique is one that I 'channeled' for a client. It involves entering Extended Me Time while staring at yourself in a mirror. Narcissism, by the way, is not advised when practicing this technique!

First, you enter the eyes-open meditative state, but this time by using your reflection as the object of your attention. You look right at the centre of your eyes, and then imagine you are observing yourself from the back of your eyeballs. Without moving your eyes, let your awareness drift to the edges of the mirror, and then the wall, or the room, around the mirror. Let time soften.

Allow the version of you from a few years earlier to appear in front of you, perhaps with fewer wrinkles, and let a smile cross your lips. Then, while that younger version of you stares back at you, allow yourself to densify back into 'the Now'.

This either works because you are morphically resonating with an earlier version of yourself, or because it makes you relaxed—or some mix of both. I should emphasise that I don't use the technique myself and that you can do it just with your imagination and without a mirror. Just allow the version of you that you are projecting to be that 'earlier you'. It is safe to do, though, and seems to work.

No Time at All

To enter the first level of any meditation, the easiest method is to centre your attention on a singular 'thing'. This could be your breath, a mantra, some music or, with your eyes open, an object like a candle flame or just a spot on the wall. From this light meditative state, you become an observer of your thoughts, and our thoughts collapse in on themselves when we 'think' about them.

This takes us to a deeper state, which can often be reached when listening to guided meditations. It is also the state where we enter Extended Me Time.

From this deep state, we can move our consciousness from our head to other areas of our body, and to points outside our body. I use this technique in my jet lag visualisation, for example.

Several years ago, in a group meditation, I was led through this technique. The workshop leader used the gentle beating of a drum to induce a relaxed state. We were all lying down, yet I detected, from the lack of any snoring, that nobody had fallen asleep.

I found myself in a strange place. A swirling purple void where I was enveloped in love. I just wanted to stay there and not come back. It felt like I had come 'Home'. When I opened my eyes, everything I saw seemed brighter, and sounds seemed crisper, sharper, and cleaner.

I saw a documentary some years later about the early stages of the Universe. To show what the post-Big-Bang Universe looked like before light was created, when there was 'no time at all', the documentary contained an animation of a swirling mass of particles in constant motion, bouncing into each other.

I was immediately reminded of what I experienced during this meditation.

Living Weller Longer

We live in a world where it appears time is in control and marches forward relentlessly. My hope for this book is that it changes your view of time and allows you to take time under a better degree of control. The examples in this last quarter, and specifically this last chapter, illustrate some of the slightly stranger things that can happen if we play with time. While reversing the time flow might be beyond our capabilities, we can certainly slow its passage down so we can get more done with less of it.

When we introduce the practice of mindfulness meditation into our lives, we open the door to increasing our well being, and even to extending our longevity. So not only do we better manage our time by how we allow each second to pass by, but we also give ourselves more seconds to enjoy. The sooner we start a time-full existence, the more we may potentially benefit over our whole lifetime. Such benefits are of course circular. If we can live longer, it makes sense that we also enjoy a good quality of life for any additional years we might generate.

I will leave you with a temporal mantra for you to ponder and meditate upon ...

'Be mindful, timeful, and kindful and, at all times, remember that slowing down is the new speeding up.'

Timeful Task : 10 Minutes of Me Time

EACH AND EVERY DAY, TAKE 10 MINUTES OUT, EITHER TO MEDITATE OR JUST TO GO FOR A WALK.

When we learn to enter Extended Me Time, it pays back many times over in temporal dividends.

This time comes right back to us and is not time that is wasted as it will lead to us living weller for longer.

It is the best time management technique ever and both simple and free.

Twelve Temporal Takeaways

THANK YOU FOR INVESTING YOUR VALUABLE TIME AND MAKING IT TO THE END OF THIS BOOK.

Like all journeys, it pays dividends to look back on where you've been to realise where you have ended up. My hope is that you will see time in a different light and cherish each and every moment on this special planet.

By way of summary, and to save you time, here are the key takeaways from this book:

Quarter 1 : First Tickings

I : We are the creators of our own lack of time
II : It is nonsense to measure the age of the Universe in years
III : How our system of time came about

Quarter 2 : Perceptions of Time

IV : Our left and right brains experience time differently

V : Time is different for other parts of our neurology

VI : The passage of time is subjective

Quarter 3 : Managing Time

VII : The importance of Me Time

VIII : Synchronising with Natural Time

IX : Allowing everything to arrive Just in Time

Quarter 4 : Temporal Alchemy

X : How the past impinges on our efficiency in the Now

XI : Entangling with the perfect Future You

XII : Time is a dimension that can be manipulated

A Picture Tells 30,000 Words

For those who are pictorially stimulated, here's the Mind Map version I mentioned in Chapter IV: Two Minds of Time. Notice how it starts top right and the flow goes clockwise around the map. In one glance, with our right brain, we are able to see the whole book, its flow and structure. Our left brains can then zoom in and take in the detail.

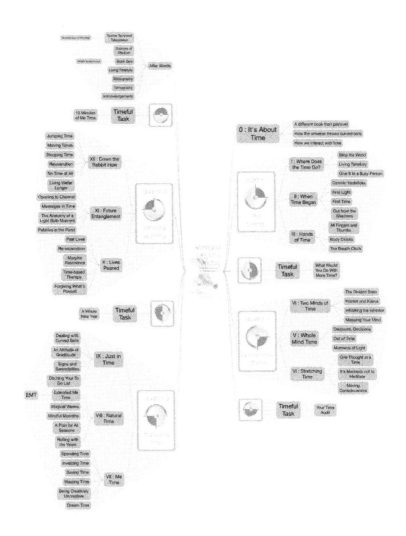

.

Sources of Wisdom

THIS IS A BOOK OF TEMPORAL DELIGHTS. SOME OF IT CONSISTS OF FUTURE MEMORIES AND ANCIENT WISDOM THAT I HAVE 'CHANNELLED' FROM THE COLLECTIVE MIND. SOME OF THE CONTENTS I HAVE COLLATED FROM A SERIES OF BOOKS I CAN HIGHLY RECOMMEND FOR THOSE WHO WANT TO KNOW MORE. I MAKE NO APOLOGIES FOR INCLUDING SOME OF MY BOOKS IN THIS LIST.

For a non-technical explanation of how scientists work out how far away everything is, read *Measuring the Universe* by Kitty Ferguson.

Get a copy of *Time* by Alexander Waugh to discover how humankind came up with our current calendar and time system.

Read *Making Time* by Steve Taylor for an exploration on the subjectivity of our perception of time.

For a fictional account of how we started to measure time and have now become so time poor, read *The Timekeeper* by Mitch Albom.

If you want to tap into future memories and learn how to become prescient and precogniscent, check out my book *The Art and Science of Light Bulb Moments*.

For an expansive explanation of the divided brain, take a month out and curl up to *The Master and His Emissary* by the brilliant Iain McGilchrist. If you haven't got a month to spare, Google "Divided Brain, Iain McGilchrist" and you'll find an excellent 12-minute animated YouTube video that explains it all much better than I ever could.

For a wonderful journey into what it is like to be entrapped in lower dimensions, read *Flatland: A Romance of Many Dimensions* by Edwin Abbott—or better still, check out one of the many animated movies.

For an exploration of what science doesn't really know, just yet, read *The Science Delusion* by the wonderfully maverick, Rupert Sheldrake.

For a metaphysical and probably more accurate explanation of how we came to be on this special planet, put all your previous beliefs on hold and read *Cosmic Memory* by Rudolph Steiner. You will see that he describes what we now call accretions discs as the 'Saturn Phase' of the Universe, years ahead of when they were seen by telescopes. He also, perhaps unwittingly, describes how the Earth and Moon were formed by a proto-planetary collision in the early stage of our Solar System.

If you want to change the way you look at the Sun, Moon, and stars—and the space in between—check out *The Self-Aware Universe* by Amit Goswami.

To catch up with how science is embracing the integration of consciousness with its models, read *Science and the Akashic Field* by Ervin László.

To get your head around why we are nine-dimensional spirits having a three-dimensional experience, played out over the dimension of time, read my book *Planes of Being*. You may also like its prequel *Flavours of Thought*.

For some leading-edge scientific thinking, including how gravity and time are interlinked, read *What a Wonderful World* by Marcus Chown.

Read *Herstoria* by Wendy Salter and *Cloud Atlas* by David Mitchell for two fictional explorations on how the future, past, and present are inextricably intertwined.

To learn more about how the past and future can be manipulated from the present, read *Create Your Perfect Future* by Anne Jirsch and *Future Memory* by PMH Atwater.

And last but not least, *What My Soul Told Me* by Richard Barrett didn't exactly provide source material, as such, for this book, but it provided the impetus for me to write a different book from the one my ego-mind had planned.

The content of the last quarter on Temporal Alchemy was, in particular, something I did not aim to share quite yet. My soul obviously had other plans.

Thanks to all the brilliant minds that planted such fruitful seeds in mine. Keep shining, whether you are on the Earth Plane or elsewhere.

10 Minutes of Mindfulness

IF YOU'D LIKE TO MEDITATE, BUT DON'T KNOW HOW, THREE MEDITATIVE VISUALISATIONS ACCOMPANY THIS BOOK TO HELP YOU EXPERIENCE THE STATE OF 'MIND-FULL-NESS'.

I am passionate about getting the whole world to take 10 minutes of me time out each day so they are free for readers of this series of books.

Meditation 1: 10 Minutes of Mindfulness

This meditation takes just 10 minutes to listen to, ideally in the morning, and is the perfect tonic to set you up for the most amazing day ahead.

Meditation 2: Be Calm

This visualisation takes you through the most common ways to make your mind go quiet—by meditating on a mantra, on the breath, and on thought itself.

Meditation 3: Noticing Time

This sample visualisation, from my Living Timefully program and workshop, demonstrates how the passage of time is subjective.

Use the code MTK100 on checkout to get access to them completely free.

http://www.tomevans.co/10-minutes-of-mindfulness/

And, for even more karma points, leave a review on Amazon, as what goes around comes around!

Book Zero : Mindful Timeful Kindful

THIS BOOK IS AN INTRODUCTION TO MINDFULNESS AND TO MINDFULNESS MEDITATION

In addition to exploring the benefits to our health and well being, I explain how we can use the practice of mindfulness meditation to get real world results.

Just imagine then that by meditating for just 10 minutes every day, you could improve not just your health but increase your wealth too.

Just imagine if you could generate more time and give both your creativity and productivity a boost.

Just imagine being luckier in life and in luck.

Just imagine stepping into a new way of being in just 21 days.

Mindful Timeful Kindful is the intentionally short and inexpensive book in a new series that will show you how to do this and more.

Available in print and for ereaders from
www.tomevans.co/books

Living Timefully

THERE ARE SEVERAL OPTIONS AVAILABLE FOR THOSE WHO ARE KEEN TO FURTHER EXPLORE THE TEMPORAL POTENTIALITIES EXPLORED IN THIS BOOK.

My Living Timefully self-study course takes you on a temporal journey over 10 weeks that goes into this subject matter in much more detail. You will actually experience time dilation and even time shifts as a result.

If you just want your days to go smoother, I have selected five of the meditative visualisations from the full Living Timefully course and they are available in the 'Your Perfect Day' pack of meditations.

If you are interested in training as a Living Timefully Practitioner, you will also find details here.

www.livingtimefully.com

Tom Evans

Tomography

TOM EVANS IS AN EX-BBC TV ENGINEER WHO BECAME AN AUTHOR BY ACCIDENT IN HIS MID-40S, AFTER DISCOVERING HOW TO MEDITATE.

These days, his writing has become a full-time occupation, and he is also the host of the popular podcast, The Zone Show.

His clients refer to him with many monikers such as thebookwright, the wizard of lightbulb moments, and temporal alchemist.

From Tom's perspective, he still doesn't know what he wants to be when he grows up.

Find out more at www.tomevans.co

Follow him on Twitter at
www.twitter.com/thebookwright

Tom Evans

Bibliography

Non-fiction Titles

Blocks
The Art and Science of Light Bulb Moments
Flavours of Thought
Planes of Being
The Zone
This We Know
This We Are
New Magic for a New Era

Short Stories

One Hundred Years of Ermintrude
Soulwave
The Germinatrix

Tom Evans

Acknowledgements

AS WITH ALL PROJECTS, THIS SERIES OF BOOKS
WOULD NOT HAPPEN IF IT WASN'T FOR SEEDS AND
ASSISTANCE PROVIDED BY OTHER PEOPLE.

So, big thanks to TheCreativePenn, Joanna Penn, for
giving me the seed idea to create a series of books on
practical mindfulness.

Thanks to Harmony Kent for massaging my words into
something that makes better sense.

Thanks to Steve Palfreyman for helping me get all the
ducks in a row over the last few moonths.

Thanks to Tina Fotherby for helping me shine my light
in this latest orbit of the Sun.

Thanks to Doug New for the continuing magical
support.

To Louise, as always, for giving me time and space.

Lightning Source UK Ltd.
Milton Keynes UK
UKOW06f0959120617

303161UK00016B/849/P